ID0474438

WELL NO ONE'S EVER COMPLAINED BEFORE . . .

OR HOW TO BE MORE ASSERTIVE

Judith Stewart originally trained and worked as a careers officer. She is now a freelance trainer and writer. She runs courses both in industry and in the public sector specialising in assertiveness, counselling, interviewing techniques and working with groups. Judith admits to having been a very non-assertive person who has gradually learned to change her life by becoming assertive.

WELL NO ONE'S EVER COMPLAINED BEFORE . . .

OR HOW TO BE MORE ASSERTIVE

Judith Stewart

Illustrations by Shaun Williams

ELEMENT BOOKS

© Judith Stewart 1989

First published in 1989 by
Element Books Limited
Longmead, Shaftesbury, Dorset

Designed by Jenny Liddle
Cover illustration by Shaun Williams
Cover design by Max Fairbrother
Typeset by Photoprint, Torquay, Devon
Printed and bound in Great Britain by
Billings Ltd, Hylton Road, Worcester

British Library Cataloguing in Publication Data
Stewart, Judith
Well no one's ever complained before – .
1. Self-assertion
I. Title
158'.1
ISBN 1–85230–082–5

CONTENTS

ACKNOWLEDGEMENTS   vii

CHAPTER ONE. **ASSERTIVE BEHAVIOUR**   1

In which we are introduced to Mark and Helen and
their mysterious friend Chris, and Mark and Helen
learn about assertive behaviour.

CHAPTER TWO. **RETURNING FAULTY GOODS**   13

In which Mark and Helen learn how to return the
faulty toaster assertively.

CHAPTER THREE. **SAYING NO**   23

In which Mark and Helen learn how to say *no*
assertively to friends and colleagues.

CHAPTER FOUR. **REACHING A COMPROMISE**   35

In which Mark and Helen learn about negotiation,
and Helen discovers how to reach a compromise with
her mother, who wants to stay for Easter.

CHAPTER FIVE. **DEALING WITH CRITICISM**   48

In which Mark and Helen learn how to accept

criticism assertively, and Mark finds out how to deal with his difficult boss.

CHAPTER SIX. **MORE ON CRITICISM** 60

In which Mark and Helen learn how to deal with put-downs, and discover how to give criticism.

CHAPTER SEVEN. **RELATIONSHIPS** 69

In which Mark and Helen discover how to use assertiveness to deal with anger and grudges and to improve close relationships.

CHAPTER EIGHT. **THE INTERVIEW** 83

In which Chris helps Helen with a job application, and Helen learns how to be assertive in an interview.

FINALE 95

In which the tables are turned.

HELEN'S SUGGESTED READING LIST 97

ACKNOWLEDGEMENTS

With very many thanks to all those people who influenced this book. To Mike Woods who gave me the original idea and the courage to write it, and to Kenneth Blanchard and Spencer Johnson who provided the inspiration for the style. To Derek Close and Rowena Hargreaves, Chris and Jackie Eling, Sasha Fenton, Dr David Lindsay, Naomi Ozaniec and Peter Stewart for all their invaluable help and advice. To Barrie Hopson who first introduced me to assertiveness and to Brenda Allcock and Jude Higgins and all the authors of the books in Helen's reading list who have helped me to become more assertive. And last but not least to Steve Eddy for all his editorial work and to my commissioning editor Simon Franklin who gave me so much help and encouragement.

To T.T.

nce upon a time Mark and Helen
bought a toaster . . .

CHAPTER ONE

ASSERTIVE BEHAVIOUR

In which we are introduced to Mark and Helen and their mysterious friend Chris, and Mark and Helen learn about assertive behaviour.

*   *   *   *   *

'So why did you buy it if you didn't want it?' Mark shouted from the hall.

Helen didn't hear the question, she was already in the kitchen making coffee. 'Well I suppose now that we've bought it we might as well use it.'

She turned on the toaster and put in a couple of pieces of bread. A few minutes later there was a smell of burning and smoke started to rise from the toaster.

'I thought that the assistant said that it toasted all types of bread,' she muttered to herself, rather puzzled. 'Mark,' she called, 'I'm having problems with the toaster. I've only put it on a low setting and it's burnt the toast.'

Mark came into the kitchen and went over to the smoking toaster. He unplugged it, pulled out the burnt pieces of toast and fiddled with the controls.

'That'll probably work now,' he said confidently. 'Let's try another piece of bread.'

His forehead wrinkled in frustration as, once again, the toast started to burn. 'The stupid thing doesn't work,' he said angrily, 'it's not popping up. Where are the instructions?'

He spent a couple of moments reading through the booklet. 'Okay, we certainly don't seem to be doing anything wrong, it must be a faulty toaster. Let's have one more go and try the sliced bread this time.'

Yet again the kitchen filled with the smell of burning toast. 'Damn, it's definitely faulty, Helen, we're going to have to take it back!'

*　　*　　*　　*　　*

'Burning the baked beans again Mark?' said a cheery voice from the kitchen door, 'How did the shopping trip go, or shouldn't I ask?'

'Oh hi, Chris,' said Helen, 'Come in and have a cup of coffee. Everything was going fine until I went to buy the toaster . . . '

Chris perched on one of the kitchen stools. 'What happened?'

'Well, I went into the electrical shop on the High Street to look at toasters. I'd read about one recently that sounded particularly good value for money.

'The assistant didn't have that model in stock, but he kept bringing out toaster after toaster. Before I knew it he had almost every toaster in the shop out on the counter. The shop was very busy, there was a queue of people waiting to be served and everybody seemed to be looking at me. I got more and more embarrassed and in the end I felt that it was easier to buy one than to say no.'

'Couldn't you have told the assistant that you didn't like any of the toasters?' asked Chris.

'You know what it's like – the assistant had gone to so much trouble to get all those toasters out and seemed to expect me to buy one, I didn't want to make a fuss. Afterwards I felt such a fool that I'd ended up with a toaster I didn't want. I even started to feel angry with the assistant.'

'Yes, I know what you mean,' said Chris wryly, 'I used to be the same. I had great trouble saying no to sales

2

assistants and always felt obliged to buy something. It all came to a head one day when I went into a shop to look at personal stereos. At that stage I was only *thinking* about buying one and I wanted to shop around to see what was available.

'The first shop I went into had one that I liked. The sales assistant said that it was the last day of their sale and they only had a couple left. Instead of saying that I'd like to look in a few more shops before making up my mind, which is what I had intended to do, I allowed myself to be pressurised by the sales assistant and I bought it. Later that day I came across a much better model for the same price!'

'That evening I was telling a friend what had happened and how annoyed I was with myself. He'd been on a couple of assertiveness training courses and explained that one of the things he'd learned was how to handle similar situations and how to say no without feeling guilty. I decided to find out about assertiveness for myself and it's really made a difference.'

'Assertive – ' interrupted Mark, 'isn't that just another word for being very domineering and selfish?'

'A lot of people do think that,' Chris agreed, 'but really that's aggressive, not assertive behaviour.'

'What do you mean?' asked Helen.

'Well,' explained Chris, 'when we meet any situation that makes us anxious most of us tend to behave aggressively or non-assertively. These types of situations vary from person to person. Some people, like you Helen, are very nervous when they feel they're under pressure to buy something. Others have difficulties saying no to friends, colleagues or parents, and many of us get anxious when dealing with people in authority.

'In stressful situations some people respond aggressively. This doesn't necessarily mean that they shout and scream, but they verbally attack the other person and aim to win, getting their own way regardless. Aggressive people state what they want or feel very strongly. Often they

3

AN AGGRESSIVE PERSON TAKING THE TOASTER
BACK MIGHT SHOUT AT THE SALESPERSON AS
IF THEY WERE PERSONALLY RESPONSIBLE FOR
THE FAULT...

will put the other person down and belittle their beliefs or needs – the type of person who says that you are stupid if you don't feel or think as they do. Aggressive people fight for their own rights but ignore that others have rights too. They are often good at making decisions about their own lives but then tend to impose those decisions on others.

'In the case of your toaster, an aggressive person taking it back would probably slam it down on the counter, exaggerate the problem out of all proportion, and have a row with the sales assistant as if they were personally responsible for the fault.'

'I used to have a boss like that when I was training as an accountant,' said Mark. 'He used to shout at me if I ever made the slightest mistake. I can picture him now, he used to come into my office, stand there with his arms folded and then proceed to tell me how stupid and incompetent I was and that I'd better pull my socks up. Afterwards I used to feel *so* humiliated and angry.

'Mind you, I can be aggressive myself,' he continued with a wry smile. 'Although I do behave passively in some situations, my normal reaction is to be aggressive, but I nearly always feel guilty about it later.'

'Yes,' Chris nodded, 'being aggressive often leaves us feeling bad afterwards even if we won at the time, and being on the receiving end of aggressive behaviour can leave us feeling very hurt and resentful.

'On the other hand, non-assertive behaviour is not necessarily any better; the person who tends to behave non-assertively wants to run away from conflict or confrontation. They don't stand up for their rights and tend to let others make decisions for them rather than say what *they* want to do. They have difficulty expressing their needs and feelings and they are often so indirect in asking for anything that they never get their message across.'

'Like my mother,' interrupted Helen, 'she asks for things in such a roundabout way that I never know what she wants and if I ask her what she wants to do, she says,

5

"I don't mind dear, you choose, I'll fit in with you." If we go out for a meal with her she always asks us first what we're having to eat or drink before she'll choose hers. It drives Mark and me mad, especially when things don't go well and she seems to think that it's our fault because we chose the restaurant or the meal.'

'I get so angry,' added Mark, 'because she will never say what she really wants and I resent having to do all the work and make the decisions for her.'

'That's the whole point,' Chris agreed. 'Non-assertive people always want to fit in with the wishes of others; they don't like to hurt or upset anyone. They don't realise how maddening their behaviour can be. Because they don't say what they want, you have to guess and if you guess wrongly then it can easily happen that *no one* gets what they want.

'A non-assertive person returning your toaster would probably tentatively approach the sales assistant and almost apologise for returning it, as if they had done something wrong in buying a faulty toaster in the first place. In describing the problem they are likely to understate the case. They may well accept whatever the shop offers even if that means having the toaster repaired, although they may legally be entitled to a refund.

'Another thing non-assertive people tend to do is to put themselves down. They say things like, "You know how stupid I am about electrical things," "I'm so hopeless when it comes to money," or "I can't cook to save my life." Putting yourself down like this is a particularly bad thing to do because if you tell people that you are not good at something the chances are that they'll believe you. It's very important to learn not to belittle yourself, and on some assertiveness courses they help people to do this by calling "foul" every time someone puts themselves down.'

'I can certainly recognise some of my own behaviour there,' admitted Helen. 'When I'm anxious I tend to be non-assertive, although occasionally I blow my top and get really angry.'

6

'That's an important point,' Chris replied. 'Although we tend on the whole to behave either aggressively or non-assertively, most of us can flip from one behaviour to the other, and we may be aggressive in some situations and non-assertive in others.'

'Like Mother again,' mused Helen. 'Although she's non-assertive with friends and with people in authority she can be really aggressive in other situations. She was never non-assertive with me when I was a child, quite the opposite in fact.'

'I know what you mean,' nodded Chris, 'my mother was the same. However, we don't have to behave like that – there is another way of behaving, a middle path which allows us to say what we really want and still respect the wishes of others.'

'You mean assertiveness,' said Helen.

'Exactly,' said Chris. 'Assertive behaviour is all about equality. The assertive person is not out to win regardless of the consequences. They can say clearly what they think, feel, or what they want to happen, but in a way that considers the wishes of others. Whereas both non-assertive and aggressive behaviour come from a feeling of low self-esteem, assertive behaviour comes from high self-esteem.

'Assertive people stand up for their rights but not at the expense of the rights of others. They are decisive, making choices about their own lives without forcing those choices onto others. Assertiveness isn't necessarily about getting your own way – it's about communicating honestly and directly, but if you say what you want assertively, then you're more likely to get it than if you behave non-assertively or aggressively.

'A person on the receiving end of assertive behaviour is likely to feel as though they've been respected and treated equally.'

'Are you telling us that aggressive or non-assertive behaviour is always wrong?' interjected Mark. 'Because I

7

can think of all sorts of situations where aggression may be the best way to behave.'

'You're absolutely right Mark, I'm not saying they're always wrong. It usually *is* better to behave assertively, but there are occasions when one of the other behaviours may be more sensible. For example, if you come across a crowd of people standing round a road accident, then you may have to take control and tell people what to do in order to make sure that the crowd moves, someone phones for help, and you can give the injured person first aid. Although you could do this politely you would certainly be behaving aggressively rather than assertively.

'The skill of assertive behaviour is being able to assess a situation, consider the consequences and then behave appropriately.'

'So how could I have behaved assertively when I bought the toaster?' Helen asked tentatively.

'Before we can behave assertively we have to accept that we all have certain rights. For instance, **we all have the right to say no, without feeling guilty**.

'In your case Helen, if you didn't want to buy any of the goods the sales assistant showed you, then it's a question of accepting your right to say no, and if you feel under an obligation because they've been very helpful then you can always say something that acknowledges that help but you don't have to buy anything.'

'You mean something like, "I appreciate all the trouble you've gone to but none of these toasters is quite what I want." '

'Absolutely,' Chris agreed, 'that way neither of you will feel bad. You haven't ended up with a toaster you don't want, and the assistant's hard work has been acknowledged and appreciated. If you really feel bad about saying no then you may well find it helpful to say so. I certainly do in that sort of situation, I tend to say, "I feel really bad saying this after you've been so helpful, but I don't like any of these toasters" – or whatever it is.

9

'On the other hand, if you weren't sure whether you wanted one of the toasters or not then you could have bought some time to make your decision. When we're under pressure we often feel obliged to make a decision on the spot, but one of the skills of assertiveness is asking for time to think about what you want to do. If you had felt that you wanted time to think about it, maybe to read a consumer report, or ask friends, then you could have said just that.

'Remember though that assertiveness is being honest, not a way of making excuses. If you really don't want one of the toasters, say so.'

'Are you saying that assertiveness is simply knowing what you want and then asking for it without forcing the choice on the other person?' asked Mark.

'That is certainly a large part of assertive behaviour,' Chris replied, 'accepting our right **to ask for what we want, always bearing in mind that the other person has a right to say no**, and then asking for it in a clear concise way. But, knowing what you want is often the hardest part of being assertive.'

'No wonder I'm not very assertive,' mused Helen, 'I've always had trouble asking for what I wanted. I remember my mother saying, "Those who ask don't get. Those who don't ask, don't want." When Mark and I got married she didn't approve of the idea of us having a wedding present list because she felt that if people were good enough to buy us a present it should be what they wanted to buy us – even if it meant us having ten irons!

'So, having said all that what do I do about my toaster?' she continued.

'Well Helen, there are various techniques that will help and I'll be delighted to run through them with you. First of all though, I've got a couple of things to sort out at home. Why don't we meet in the Coach and Horses later this evening?'

'That would be fine Chris – we'll look forward to it. I

think before then I'd better write some of this down,' said Helen, 'you know what my memory's like.'

'Foul,' yelled Chris and Mark together.

'What did I do?' asked Helen, looking bewildered.

'You put yourself down for having a bad memory,' said Chris.

'Okay,' said Helen with a smile, 'I'll go and write some of this down so that I can remind myself later of what you've said!' And with that she went to get her notebook . . .

Helen's Notebook

THERE ARE 3 WAYS OF BEHAVING:

AGGRESSIVE — aims to 'win' regardless of the other person.

NON-ASSERTIVE — avoids conflict or confrontation even if it means the other person 'wins'.

ASSERTIVE — states clearly and honestly what they want, think and feel but also considers others.

Perhaps the hardest part of assertiveness is knowing what you want.

Assertiveness means accepting certain rights:

* The right to say NO without feeling guilty

* The right to say what we want, bearing in mind that the other person has a right to say no.

DON'T PUT YOURSELF DOWN!

CHAPTER TWO

RETURNING FAULTY GOODS

In which Mark and Helen learn how to return the faulty toaster assertively.

*   *   *****   *   *

That evening . . .

'Right,' said Chris, as they all settled down round a log fire in the village pub, 'you wanted to look at some techniques to help you be assertive when you take the toaster back.'

'That's right,' Helen nodded. 'Since we saw you this afternoon we've checked a few things. We contacted our local consumer advice people and were told that if the toaster was faulty, we were entitled to get our money back.'

Mark continued, 'We've read the instructions very carefully to make sure that it *is* the toaster that's faulty and not us doing something wrong. It would be really embarrassing to take it back only to find out that it was our fault it wasn't working. We've also made sure that we've got the receipt.'

'While I was on the phone to the consumer advice people,' Helen added, 'I also asked what would have happened if the toaster hadn't been faulty, but that when we'd got it home we realised that we just didn't like it. We were surprised to discover that although shops don't have to exchange goods, many of them would.'

13

'Well,' said Chris. 'I was going to say that the first stages in assertiveness are to decide on what you want and then to find out whether that is realistic, but you've beaten me to it. You've done a lot of the homework, which is so important because there's no point in asking assertively for something that would be quite unrealistic to expect.

'The other thing I was going to say was that when it comes to practising assertiveness it's sensible to start with a situation that is relatively straightforward, gradually building up to more difficult ones as your confidence develops. Returning your faulty toaster to a shop is an ideal situation to start with.

'So,' Chris continued, 'now you've decided on what you want to achieve and checked that it is reasonable, the next stage is to work out what you want to say and who you need to speak to.'

'I presume we might as well talk to the manager,' said Mark. 'There's no point in explaining it all to a sales assistant who probably can't make a decision.'

'I would agree,' Chris nodded. 'When it comes to explaining the problem, the skill of doing that assertively is to keep calm, look the other person in the eye and tell them clearly and concisely what is wrong – don't waffle. When people are anxious they often pad out what they want to say with things like: "I'm not too sure how to say this but . . . ", "What I'm trying to say is . . . ", "I'm terribly sorry to bother you but . . . " and this can obscure what they're really trying to say.'

Helen thought for a moment. 'So I could say to the manager: "I bought this toaster a couple of days ago. It doesn't work properly so I'd like a refund please." '

'That's fine,' said Chris. 'If it's a good, reputable shop, that's probably all you'll need to do. You've only got a problem if the shop has a policy of avoiding giving refunds. Then they're likely to do everything possible to dissuade you from taking a refund. This is where other assertiveness techniques come in.

14

'The most important thing is not to get drawn into an argument or to get sidetracked, but to hold your own position. There are two assertiveness techniques for doing this. They're called **broken record** and **fielding**.

'The first one of these, broken record, is simply to keep repeating your message, like a record with the needle stuck, until the other person hears you. I use this technique if I'm at a party and someone asks me to drink when I'm driving. I just keep repeating, "Thank you but I don't drink and drive." If they argue and tell me that just one won't hurt me, I don't get into the argument of whether just one is going to cause any harm or not. I just keep saying "No thank you, I don't drink any alcohol if I'm driving." '

'Now, on its own this technique does work but it is very stilted and the other person may feel that you're not listening to them, so in most situations you'll need to use this along with another assertiveness technique. That's where fielding comes in. This is a way of listening and responding to the other person without being drawn into an argument.'

'Fielding means acknowledging that you've heard what they're saying, repeating some of their own words, and in some cases you may well empathise with their point of view but you then repeat your broken record. Suppose the assistant says, "This is a very reliable model and no one's ever complained before about these toasters." You could say, "This model may normally be very reliable but this particular one is definitely faulty and I would like a refund." '

'I can see what you're getting at,' said Helen. 'Could we possibly have a practice? I hope I won't meet any difficulties when I take it back, but let's just act it out as if the shop were going to do everything possible to stop me getting a refund.'

'Good idea,' said Chris. 'Okay, I'm the manager of the electrical shop. You've just come in carrying the toaster.

15

*   *   *   *   *

'Can I help you madam?'

'Yes please. I bought this toaster a couple of days ago; it's faulty and I'd like a refund.'

'That's very strange madam, this model is known for its reliability, no one's ever complained before.'

'You may not have had any complaints before but this particular toaster is faulty and I'd like a refund.'

'But madam can't have read the instructions properly – these toasters are never faulty.'

'I have read and followed the instructions very carefully. It is a faulty toaster.'

'Do you normally have problems with electrical things madam?'

Helen hesitated looking puzzled, then took a deep breath and said, 'I'm not talking about other electrical goods, I'm talking about this toaster, which is definitely faulty.'

'Well, what exactly is the problem madam?'

'The pop-up mechanism doesn't work and the toast burns.'

'Oh very well, I'd better take a look at it. Yes madam, this toaster does seem to be faulty. We'll send it away to be repaired. It'll probably take about three weeks.'

'No,' said Helen. 'I don't want it repairing, I'd like my money back.'

'Tell you what, if you don't want it repaired we could let you choose another toaster.'

'No thank you,' said Helen, 'I'd like my money back.'

'I'm sorry madam I can't do that. As a matter of policy we don't give refunds, but we can give you a replacement or a credit note. Perhaps if you don't want another toaster you'd like to choose something else in the shop.'

16   'Thank you, I don't want anything else in the shop. This toaster is faulty and you are legally obliged to give me my money back.'

'Very well, if madam would like to come with me to the cash desk I'll sort out the paperwork.'

*   *   *****   *   *

'That was really good Helen,' said Chris. 'You certainly fielded everything I said very well. How did that feel?'

'Fine,' said Helen looking pleased. 'I feel much more confident now. There's only one other thing bothering me. In situations like that I get really nervous. Is there anything I can do to help me stay calm?'

'Yes there is,' said Chris. 'I used to get very nervous too and I've gradually found ways to overcome this. I always find that doing my homework helps because then I know my legal rights or have the right information to hand, and that gives me a lot of confidence. Just before I go into any situation I'm nervous about, I stop for a moment or two and just take some very deep, slow breaths and relax my muscles – it's amazing how that calms me down.

'I also find it helpful to run through the situation in my mind first, imagining what the other person might say and how I'll respond.

'Which leads us to another of the things we need to consider when we're learning to become assertive, and that's body language. You're probably very aware of this Helen, being a teacher.'

'Yes, I certainly know how important it is,' Helen replied. 'I remember learning once that only about a quarter of what we say is conveyed by our words – the rest is conveyed by tone of voice and body language. I find that I'm very aware of it in the classroom. If a child is telling me one thing and their body language is saying something else then I believe the body language.'

Chris agreed. 'That's why it matters so much in assertiveness. If we want to say something assertive then it's important that our body language and tone of voice are also assertive. To achieve this we need to have good self-esteem

17

IF YOU DON'T BELIEVE WHAT YOU'RE
SAYING YOUR BODY LANGUAGE AND
TONE OF VOICE WILL GIVE YOU AWAY...

and to believe in what we're saying. Suppose that you were asking for a pay rise at work because you were taking on more responsibility. If you don't genuinely believe that you deserve the pay rise then you would be unlikely to convince someone else.

'In your situation with the toaster, knowing your rights helps, but you also need to believe in your ability to return the toaster successfully. If you think that your body language or tone of voice may be less than confident then learn to become aware of them and change them if necessary.'

'Why don't you and I do a role-play Mark to see how we look when we're being non-assertive or aggressive,' suggested Helen.

'I don't mind – what do you think Chris?'

'That sounds like a good idea. Okay Helen, why don't you tell Mark very non-assertively that he's left the bathroom looking really untidy and you want him to tidy it up.'

*   *   *   *   *

Helen slumped, looked at the floor and said in a small voice, 'Mark I've just been into the bathroom and I noticed that you've left the odd thing out. I'm sure you were very busy at the time and I don't want to be a nuisance, but could you possibly put them away sometime?'

*   *   *   *   *

'Fine,' said Chris – 'Mark, what did you notice about Helen's body language and tone of voice?'

'Well,' said Mark, 'she didn't look me in the eye once and her posture was very slouched. She kept fiddling with her ring, twisting it round her finger and it was difficult to hear her because her voice was so quiet.'

'Good,' said Chris, 'Okay Mark it's your turn now. Let's try the same thing, only aggressively this time.

19

*   *   *   *   *

Mark thought for a moment, then squared his shoulders. He raised his voice and said: 'Helen I'm sick and tired of going into the bathroom after you and finding everything left out. I can't spend all my time just running after you tidying up, you know. Now go and tidy it!'

*   *   *   *   *

'Right. Now apart from wanting to hit him Helen,' smiled Chris, 'what did you notice about his body posture?'

'He raised his voice, and pointed his finger at me. He certainly looked me in the eye but it felt uncomfortable because he wouldn't look away.'

'Fine,' said Chris. 'Those were very good examples of the extremes of aggressive and non-assertive body language and tone of voice. So what you need Helen when you go back to the shop is an assertive posture and tone of voice. This means looking the other person in the eye but unlike Mark, doing it so that it doesn't feel uncomfortable, keeping your shoulders straight with your body relaxed and using a firm but not aggressive tone of voice.'

'Let me try,' said Helen.

*   *   *   *   *

She stood straight and looked Mark in the eye. 'Mark,' she said in a firm voice, 'you've left the bathroom looking untidy: please will you tidy it up.'

'That's great,' said Chris. 'If you behave like that when you go back to the shop you won't have any problems.'

20

*   *   *   *   *

RETURNING FAULTY GOODS

The following week . . .

'I'm not looking forward to this,' said Helen nervously as they approached the electrical shop, 'but following Chris's suggestion of running the situation through in my mind has really helped. I've rehearsed this at least three times.'

'Can I help you?' said a voice, almost before they were through the door.

'Yes – I'd like to see the manager please.'

'Yes madam, I am the manager. What can I do for you?'

'I bought this toaster last week and it doesn't work. I'd like my money back.'

'What exactly appears to be the trouble madam?' asked the manager, looking concerned.

'The pop-up mechanism doesn't work and the toast burns.'

'Have you tried adjusting the controls?'

'Yes, I've tried the toaster on both high and low settings but it still doesn't pop up and it burns the toast.'

'I'll go and try it,' said the manager. She returned moments later. 'Yes you're quite right madam; your toaster is faulty. You can have another one if you wish, or if you'd prefer we'll give you a refund.'

'I'd really like my money back.'

'Certainly madam.'

Helen's notebook

Homework - gather information, decide on what you want to happen and consider whether it's realistic.

Decide on what you want to say; say it calmly and clearly; be specific.

Repeat the point if necessary - broken record.

Deal with the other person's responses using some of their own words, but don't argue - fielding

If nervous, use deep breathing, run through the situation in your mind first.

Keep a straight but relaxed body posture and look the other person in the eye.

CHAPTER THREE

SAYING NO

*In which Mark and Helen learn how to say no assertively to friends
and colleagues.*

*   *   *   *   *

That evening Mark and Helen were discussing their success
in returning the toaster . . .

'I'm really pleased about the toaster,' said Helen. 'It was
so much easier than I imagined. I wish I could be assertive
like that with friends and colleagues at work; it would save
me a lot of problems.'

'What do you mean?' asked Mark.

'You know how I find it so difficult to refuse to help
anyone?' she said.

'I had noticed,' he said with a rueful smile.

'Well,' she explained, 'it's really becoming a problem.
I'm so busy at work at the moment – as well as having
a bigger class which means much more work, I'm now
spending most of my lunchtimes teaching the children
to play the recorder. I don't mind that – you know how
much I enjoy my job, but I've also been under a lot of
pressure to get involved in spare-time activities. Not only
at school, but here in the village as well. People have been
trying to get me to help with jumble sales, bring-and-buy
sales and amateur dramatics, not to mention serving on
committees. Saying no makes me feel so guilty that I
tend to say yes, and now it's all getting on top of me.
If I hadn't had that wretched flu last month I could

probably cope, but that left me feeling so tired and depressed.'

'I had noticed you'd been looking very tense and weepy recently. You've had a lot to cope with in the past year or so, what with your father dying as well as our house move and all your extra work at school. Do take care you don't take on too much or you'll make yourself ill. If you're worried why don't you have a word with the doctor?'

'I have been thinking about that. It would certainly be useful to get some professional advice but I'm worried that he'll just give me tranquillisers.'

'Tell him you don't want tranquillisers.'

'That's easier said than done,' she replied. 'I don't want to antagonise him.'

'Couldn't you use the techniques Chris has taught us?'

'I suppose I could, but it's one thing taking the toaster back to a shop where I knew my rights, and quite another asserting myself with someone who knows more about the subject than I do.'

'Perhaps Chris could help,' Mark suggested.

At that moment the phone rang. Helen answered it, 'Oh hallo Chris, we were just talking about you. How are you?'

'Fine,' Chris replied, 'I was ringing to find out how you got on with the toaster.'

'Really well,' Helen answered, 'The manager was very helpful. She checked that the toaster was faulty and then gave me my money back without any argument. I didn't need to use fielding at all.

'I'm glad you rang I was just about to give you a call. There are a couple of things I'd like to talk to you about – if you've got the time, that is.'

'Certainly, I'll be only too happy to help,' Chris replied warmly. 'When?'

'How about coming round for supper one evening next week?'

'I'd enjoy that,' said Chris, 'but the only day I'm free is Tuesday.'

'Tuesday's fine. I'll look forward to seeing you then – around eight o'clock?'

'Eight it is. See you then.'

*   *   *   *   *

The following Tuesday . . .

After supper, Chris, Helen and Mark sat round a blazing fire in the sitting room.

'How are you getting on with fielding and broken record?' Chris asked.

'Not too badly,' Helen began. 'I had a chance to use both of them just the other day and it worked very well. A salesman called selling vacuum cleaners. In the past I wouldn't have answered the door because if I had I would have felt under pressure to buy something. But I kept calm and just repeated, "I don't buy anything at the door."

'He tried telling me that this was the greatest vacuum cleaner in the universe and that I couldn't buy one like it in the shops. I was able to field everything he said and then return to my broken record and after a couple of attempts he gave up. I liked the way being assertive meant that I could talk to him pleasantly without being rude and still get my point over.'

'Talking of doors, isn't that our doorbell ringing?' asked Mark, and going to answer it. Moments later he returned with Richard, a friend of theirs.

'Hallo Helen,' Richard said, coming into the sitting room. 'I've just brought you the collecting boxes and badges for the charity collection.'

'Oh good,' said Helen, 'which streets do you want us to do Richard?'

25

But Richard didn't reply: he'd just spotted Chris.

'Chris, am I glad to see you! I was going to come round to see you this evening. I desperately need some more help with this collection. I'm sure I can rely on you to help out for a couple of hours.'

'A couple of hours, is that all you need Richard?'

'Well, maybe a little longer.'

'How much longer?'

'Oh I suppose an evening or so, nothing much.'

'I'm sorry Richard, I don't want to take on any extra commitments in the next couple of weeks.'

'But it's such a worthy cause and we really need your help.'

'Yes I know it's a worthy cause and I also realise that you need help but I won't take on anything extra at present.'

'But Chris, you're always so helpful and you're such a good collector. You seem to raise more money than anyone else.'

'That's kind of you to say so, but I really don't want to take on anything extra at present.'

'You've put me in a bit of a spot,' said Richard looking aggrieved. 'I thought I could rely on your help and now I shall have to find someone else. I don't know how I'm ever going to get this collection done. Come on Chris, you must have one free evening in the next two weeks.'

'I don't like saying no to you Richard and I realise that you're in a spot but I really don't wish to commit myself to anything extra at present,' replied Chris firmly.

'Oh all right Chris, I get the point, maybe next time.'

'Fine,' said Chris. 'If I have the time I'll be only too willing to help, Richard.'

Richard stayed a few more moments to sort out with Helen and Mark where they were to collect. After he had gone, Helen turned to Chris.

'I'm so glad that happened Chris. That's exactly my problem, except unlike you I can't say no. I'm getting so overloaded with commitments because I find it difficult to say no to people who ask me to help out with their jumble sales, summer fairs or charity collections. I really admire the way you handled Richard. Can you explain how you did that?'

'Certainly,' agreed Chris, 'basically I was fielding because he used all sorts of manipulative ploys to try to get me to say yes. The whole point of using fielding was that it enabled me to hear what he was saying and even empathise with it without getting hooked by his arguments.'

'You've mentioned empathy a couple of times,' said Mark, 'but what exactly do you mean by that? Don't you mean sympathy?'

'No,' said Chris, 'Empathy and sympathy are quite different. If you sympathise with someone, you share with them how you would feel in their situation. If you empathise, you remain yourself, but see their situation as if through their eyes.'

'So,' said Mark, 'you mean that if I'm talking to someone who's just been made redundant, if I share my own feelings about how awful the situation is, then that's sympathy?'

'Absolutely,' confirmed Chris. 'On the other hand, being made redundant may be an exciting challenge to some people, and if you were empathising with them you would understand what they're feeling – whether that's terror or excitement.'

'I know you've told us the basics of fielding,' Helen persisted, 'but can you tell us more about how you dealt with Richard?'

Chris thought for a moment. 'When Richard first asked me about the collection he was very vague and gave the impression that he only wanted me to help for a few hours.'

Mark chipped in, 'My boss at work is always doing that. He says, "Could you just do this little job for me? It won't take any time at all." And I find that he's landed me with three days work!'

Chris nodded, 'I've always called that smoke-screening. You can't see what they really want, and the assertive way to deal with that is just to keep asking them exactly what they want until they tell you. Each time they're vague you just ask for precise details – "Exactly what do you want me to do?", "How long will this job take?", and so on.

'At one point, Richard tried to make me feel guilty by saying it was such a worthy cause and he needed me. Fielding here meant just accepting that it is a worthy cause and then repeating my broken record that I wasn't prepared to take on anything extra.

'When someone does this I still feel a slight twinge of guilt but I find it helpful to remind myself of my right to say no without feeling guilty.

'It can help when you're learning to say no, not to give your reasons. If I had said that I wanted some evenings to myself Richard would have argued with me, and I could have ended up having to defend myself.'

'When you were talking to him you never said you *couldn't* help – you said you *wouldn't*. Isn't that a bit rude?' asked Mark.

'If I had said I couldn't, that would have implied that circumstances outside my control were stopping me from helping. By saying I wouldn't I was taking responsibility for my decision, not blaming it on someone else.'

'He even tried flattery, didn't he,' continued Mark, 'telling you that you were such a good collector. I liked the way you thanked him for the compliment and then returned to your broken record. I really felt annoyed with him at the end though, when he started to behave so helplessly. I wanted to tell him to sort himself out and not be such a whimp.'

'I didn't,' said Helen. 'I felt sorry for him then. I wanted to rescue him from his problem and I would've had great difficulty saying no when he told us what a spot he was in.'

28

'That, no doubt, is what he wanted me to feel,' said Chris wryly. 'I used to have difficulty saying no to people but then I found an assertiveness technique that helped enormously, in fact I used it then. It means very simply just saying how you feel – "I feel awful saying this but . . . "

'I first used this when I was asking someone to return some books they had borrowed from me and I started by saying, "I feel very embarrassed saying this but I lent you some books a couple of weeks ago and now I need them, so please could you let me have them back." I felt so much better declaring how embarrassed I was.

'There is another point about Richard's final attempt to persuade me. He tried to make me take on his problem as if it was mine, saying that I'd put him in a bit of a spot and that he didn't know how he was going to get the collection finished. This raises another of our rights – **the right to choose not to get involved in other people's problems**. The collection is Richard's problem and I can choose whether or not I wish to help him with it. All too often we find that we feel obliged to take everyone else's problems on our shoulders and consequently have no time for ourselves – as you have discovered, Helen.'

'That brings me back to my problem about saying no,' said Helen. 'As I mentioned earlier I've been getting myself over-committed by helping out colleagues and friends because I haven't been able to refuse. Having watched you cope with Richard I now feel better able to say no although I will have to deal with this little inner voice that says I should please people and not ever refuse to help them.

'The other thing I wanted to ask you, Chris, is about going to my doctor. Apart from the over-commitments, I've been under a lot of stress recently. With my father dying last year, our house move last summer, the fact that work has been really busy and stressful and on top of that I've had flu. A friend of mine, who's also been going through a lot of stress, went to her doctor and found him really helpful. He talked to her about stress and together they worked out ways in which she could control it, like using relaxation techniques and going to a counsellor.

29

'My concern is that I would like to be able to ask my doctor for similar help and advice, but I'm afraid that he might just offer me tranquillisers. I'm sure that I could use broken record and fielding to make the point that I don't want tranquillisers but I don't want to antagonise him; I really would like his help in other ways. I also feel nervous because he's my doctor and someone I tend to see as an authority figure.'

'I really understand,' said Chris. 'It can be very daunting to be assertive with someone who knows more about the subject than you do. This brings us to another one of our rights, one that we need to bear in mind when dealing with people in authority, and that is **the right to be treated with respect**. Even if you don't have your doctor's qualifications you are an equal human being and have the right to be treated with respect.'

'If you do go to see him, have you any idea how you might approach getting his help?'

'I haven't really given it much thought yet,' Helen replied, 'but I suppose that what I want is to explain the problem and then ask him for his help and advice. If he does offer me tranquillisers, my broken record could be that I do want and appreciate his advice but I don't want to take tranquillisers.'

'How will you reply if he tells you that he's the doctor and he knows best?' Mark asked.

'I'll say that I know his medical knowledge is greater than mine, but it's *my* body and I don't want to take tranquillisers.'

'Good,' Chris nodded, 'it sounds as though you're happy about what you want to say. Why don't you run through it in your mind a couple of times before you go to see him, and don't forget you can use deep breathing to help you relax if you're feeling very nervous when you get there.'

'Before you go Chris, I do have one final question,' said Mark. 'It's about Richard. He's not going to think that

30

IF YOU SAY YES WHEN
YOU MEAN NO, YOU CAN END UP
RESENTING WHAT YOU'VE AGREED TO DO ...

31

you're quite the friend he thought you were. In his view, friends help him out even if they're busy. How do you cope with that?'

'I agree,' replied Chris. 'Being assertive does have its risks and in each situation you need to weigh up carefully whether it would be better to be non-assertive, or in some cases aggressive. In my view being assertive means having the choice about how you behave, not feeling compelled to behave assertively in every situation.

'In Richard's case, if I had allowed myself to agree to collect for him I might have had to let him down later because I was too busy. On the other hand I might have done the job and felt resentful the whole time. If I'd been aggressive we would both have felt bad. In that case assertive behaviour seemed the most appropriate.

'Last week I was in quite a different situation. I was taking a very senior colleague to lunch at the Castle Vaults. Normally the food is excellent but on this occasion my meal was really awful. So I was in a real dilemma. On one hand I could complain to the manager and get my meal changed, but that might have embarrassed my colleague. On the other hand I could say nothing.'

'So what did you do?' asked Helen.

Chris pulled a face: 'I decided that in this case I'd behave non-assertively, so I ate as much of the meal as possible, leaving the rest with the excuse that I'd been given too much.'

'On that note I must leave,' said Chris. 'Thank you for a delightful supper.'

'Thank *you* for all your help,' said Helen and Mark enthusiastically.

'On the way out Chris noticed a book: 'That looks interesting, I've read some others by the same author but not that one.'

32

'Borrow it if you like,' Helen said. 'I don't need it for the next couple of weeks.'

'Thank you Helen.'

'I'll go and see my doctor some time next week and let you know how I get on.'

'Good luck,' called Chris, walking down the path.

Helen's Notebook

FIELDING

Listen to what the other person says.

Acknowledge that you have heard, using some of his or her words.

Don't get hooked into their arguments.

Don't make excuses.

Repeat your point using Broken Record.

SAYING NO

Think of the consequences of not saying no.

Don't make excuses; accept responsibility for saying no.

If you feel bad saying no – say so.

RIGHTS

* To choose not to take on other people's problems.

* To be treated with respect as an equal human being.

34

CHAPTER FOUR

REACHING A COMPROMISE

In which Mark and Helen learn about negotiation and Helen discovers how to reach a compromise with her mother, who wants to stay for Easter.

* * * * *

Some weeks later . . .

'Oh Mark, I'm really worried about Easter,' said Helen with a sigh.

'You're not still worried about your mother are you?' asked Mark, looking exasperated.

'Yes I am. She's ringing today, and she's not going to be pleased about us changing our minds about having her here over the holiday. A couple of weeks ago I said we were looking forward to her visit, and now I have to tell her we've decided to go to Rome. She always makes me feel so guilty if I say no to her.'

'I thought you were getting better at saying no,' said Mark. 'I'm sure you'll cope with this, don't worry.'

'But I *am* worried Mark. I am getting more confident about saying no to people, but in this situation I don't *just* want to say no. I wish Chris was here.'

At that moment the doorbell rang. Chris was standing there clutching a book.

'I thought I'd better bring this back, Helen, in case you wanted it.'

'Oh Chris,' said Helen with a sigh of relief, 'I am glad to see you: my mother's ringing soon and I have to tell her that she can't come for Easter because Mark and I are off to Italy. I'm really feeling guilty about saying no and I'm not too sure how to handle it.'

'Okay,' replied Chris. 'Do you want to sit down and talk it through?'

'Thank you, that would be helpful.'

Helen and Chris sat down in the sitting room with mugs of coffee.

'Tell me all about it,' said Chris.

'Well,' Helen started, 'my mother has always spent Easter with us. This year it was all arranged that she would come as usual and then out of the blue Mark and I decided to spend Easter in Rome. I don't know how to tell her. I really feel guilty about it because she's done so much for me that I feel that I shouldn't let her down. I always have this problem with her and invariably I feel so bad that I give in and do exactly what she wants.'

'I do understand,' said Chris. 'As we discussed last time, many of us find it incredibly difficult to say no to anyone. We seem to feel that if we say no and don't do what people want, we will lose their love or friendship. Women in particular tend to find it very difficult because they've often been brought up to please others and put their own interests last.

'Have you been having any success saying no to all those extra commitments since we last met?'

'Yes, I'm certainly getting better,' Helen replied. 'I keep repeating to myself that I have a right to say no without feeling guilty, which is helping. The first chance I had to put it into practice was when another teacher at school asked me to help with a bring-and-buy sale on a Saturday that I'd planned to have as a rest day. Since seeing my doctor and getting advice about dealing with my stress, I've been giving myself some weekend days off when I just relax and do things I want to, like spending a day reading, gardening or going to an art gallery with Mark.

'Well, this particular Saturday I was going to spend most of the day reading a good book. I also thought that if the weather was nice I might do a couple of hours gardening. But I was brought up to be always busy doing something, so when she asked me to help I felt really guilty saying no. It was almost like having a voice inside saying it's selfish to take a day off for myself.'

'I had to use quite a lot of self-talk to convince myself that it was all right to say no and that I shouldn't feel guilty. I told her that I *did* feel bad saying no, and that really helped, and then I said firmly that I wanted to keep that Saturday free. I didn't give any reasons why and so didn't get into any arguments about why I couldn't.'

'How did she react?' asked Chris.

'That's the surprising thing,' Helen responded. 'She told me not to worry, she could easily find someone else. She then went on to say that it was very refreshing to find someone being honest. She said that a lot of people said "Yes" and then rang her up at the last minute with an excuse about why they couldn't come. That really gave my confidence a boost and since then I've been finding it easier and easier to say no.'

'Good,' agreed Chris. 'It does happen that the more assertive you are the more confident you become; and the more confident you are the easier it is to be assertive. I've often found the same reaction from people when I've said no, because then they know where they stand, you aren't holding out hope that maybe you might, or saying you will and then backing out.'

'I have discovered one other advantage of saying no,' Helen continued, 'and that's that now I'm doing the things I want to do and can fit into my life. And I'm really enjoying them. Previously I did things out of a sense of duty or because I felt guilty saying no, and I was really resenting the time I spent on some of them.

37

BEING ASSERTIVE MEANS NOT
BEING ENSLAVED BY PARENTAL VOICES INSIDE
TELLING US WHAT WE SHOULD DO ...

'It's a sobering thought that some people may be doing the same to me, agreeing to help me out of a sense of duty or guilt rather than because they want to. I'd much rather they said no.'

Chris nodded: 'I agree, but you may well find that as you become more assertive the people around you will start to be assertive with you in return. If you are being open and honest with them they may well become open and honest with you. By the way, you mentioned that your visit to the doctor was a success. Tell me more.'

'Very well,' said Helen, 'I went along and explained about my father's death, the house move, my flu, work being very busy and all my extra commitments. I told him that I was very tense, I was crying a lot and not sleeping but that I really wanted advice on how to deal with my stress rather than a prescription for tranquillisers.'

'He explained that using tranquillisers for a short time was quite safe, and that they could well help. I had to repeat a couple of times that I really didn't want to take them before he agreed to look at other ways of dealing with stress.

'One thing that seemed to help was when I said, "I do appreciate that you're concerned for my health and that you know more about tranquillisers than I do, but I would prefer not to take them." He laughed, but in a nice way, tore up the prescription he'd already written out and jokingly said, "You *are* an awkward customer!" He then added, "Okay, let's talk about all the other ways you can deal with stress." And he was really helpful. He suggested lots of things I could do, including having some weekend days off to laze and do what I wanted, buying some good relaxation tapes and setting aside fifteen or so minutes a day to listen to the tapes and relax. He also put me in touch with a good relaxation class.'

'That *is* good Helen, especially that bit of fielding. It can help a great deal when you're saying no to someone who's trying to help you, if you can show that you realise that they really do care about your well-being.

'Right, let's get back to the problem of your mother. What are you going to do about it?'

'I'm not sure,' said Helen. 'Although I'm getting so much better at saying no, I feel that when it comes to my mother, no is a word I just can't say. I feel that I must do what she wants, and I feel so guilty about us changing our minds, yet I really want to go to Rome with Mark, so I thought I'd ask you for a bit of help.'

'Perhaps one of the first things to consider, Helen, is another of the assertiveness rights – **the right to change your mind**. Have you thought through what you want out of the situation with your mother?'

'Yes,' replied Helen, 'I really would like her to come and stay with us at any time but Easter, when I am determined to go away with Mark. It would be lovely to see her over the May bank holiday instead.'

'What you need is a **workable compromise**. This is really the art of negotiating assertively. Basically you use your normal techniques of asking for what you want clearly and concisely, using broken record if necessary to repeat your message and fielding their responses.

'Once you've made your point and as long as you feel that you won't lose any self-esteem, it may be appropriate to offer a compromise if there is one that would suit both of you. When you're talking to the other person, if you really listen carefully you may pick up clues as to what you might be able to offer as a compromise.

'Timing is very important though – if you suggest a weekend in May to your mother too early in the conversation she might feel that she's being manipulated into it, and, if it's too late, it might seem like you're just saying it to keep her quiet.'

Chris continued: 'The first time I used workable compromise was with a colleague who needed to talk to me quite a lot about her work. She had a tendency to come and see me at the most inappropriate moments and insist on talking to me then and there. I would spend time with

40

her and then get behind with my own work and feel very frustrated. After I had learned how to be assertive I decided to do something about it, but, like you, I wanted to find a compromise: I didn't just want to say no, if she wanted to see me when I was busy.

'When we sat down to discuss the problem, she said that what she really wanted was to talk to me about her work once or twice a week. She didn't always need to see me at the moment she asked, but felt that if she didn't take a stand, she might not get to see me at all. Once we had talked about what she *really* wanted, it was easy to come to a compromise of meeting once a week for lunch to talk about her work.

'One of the problems most of us have in arguments or negotiations is that when we take a stand (some negotiators call this a position), we defend it vigorously, the other person does the same, and neither of us really listens to what the other person wants (which is sometimes called their interest). Yet it's only when we can get beyond our positions and discuss our interests – what we really want out of the situation, that we can find a compromise.'

'Can you say a bit more about the difference between interest and position?' Helen asked.

'Yes.' Chris nodded, 'Perhaps one of the best examples is the one quoted in a book on negotiation called *Getting to Yes*. The authors describe two people quarrelling in a library. Both people have taken stands, or positions – one wants the window open and the other wants it closed. They argue about whether they should open the window a crack, or have it half open or a quarter open, but they can't find a solution to please them both. The librarian comes in and asks one why he wants the window open – his interest is, "to get some fresh air". She asks the other why he wants it closed and his interest is, "to avoid the draught". The librarian thinks for a moment, then opens the window in the next room, bringing in fresh air without causing a draught.'

'Mm, I see what you mean,' said Helen. 'I think my

mother's position will be that she wants to come for Easter, but her interest may be to spend a weekend with us in the spring. Although, one of her main reasons for wanting to come at Easter is that, because of the bank holidays, we have four days together rather than just the two days of any other weekend.'

'That's no problem.' Mark, who had been sitting quietly in the corner listening carefully to what Chris was saying, spoke for the first time: 'I can always take some time off work during your half-term.'

At that moment the phone rang. Helen crossed her fingers and answered it.

'Hallo Helen,' said her mother, 'how are you?'

'Fine Mother,' replied Helen. 'I'm gradually getting over this awful flu bug, although it's left me feeling very tired.'

'I've been feeling very tired recently, too, and the weather here is dreadful. It's so cold and wet – very depressing. I'm really looking forward to coming for Easter.'

'Mother, I feel really awful saying this but it won't be possible for you to come this year. Mark and I have decided to go to Italy for the holiday.'

'But I always come for Easter,' said her mother, sounding shocked.

'Yes, I know, but this year we wanted to get away on our own.'

'I shall be *so* disappointed not to come. Can't you go away another time? Have you booked yet?'

'No we haven't booked yet, and I do realise how disappointed you will be but we've made up our minds to go away for Easter.'

'Do you realise that this will be the first Easter we've spent apart since you were a little girl, I'll miss you. If you haven't booked yet, couldn't you go away another week so that I could come for Easter?'

'I do realise that this will be the first Easter we've not

43

spent together and I'll miss you too, but Mark and I have decided to go to Rome this Easter.'

'Oh well, I suppose there's nothing I can do. I'll miss seeing your garden in the spring – it looks so lovely with all the spring flowers – and I don't know what to do about having a short holiday then – I really need it.'

'There's no reason why you should miss the garden in the spring. You could come over anytime as long as it's not at Easter. Why don't you come at half-term? Mark can take a few days off and we can have a short holiday together.'

'I hadn't really thought of that. I've been coming for Easter for so long that I'd never considered coming at any other time of year. I suppose if I can't come for Easter it's the next best thing.'

'May here is lovely – the garden is at its best. All the blossom is out and perhaps if the weather is good we could have some nice country walks, maybe even a barbeque in the garden.'

'That sounds really nice. I shall look forward to coming. I hope you have a good time in Italy. Where are you going?'

'Rome.'

'I went there with your father many years ago: it's a lovely city. Don't forget to visit the catacombs – they're very interesting. I think I've still got some of my Roman guide books. I'll pop them in the post for you . . . '

Eventually Helen put the phone down looking really pleased.

'That went quite well really. She seems reasonably happy about coming in May and it will give us a chance to do some different things. Perhaps even have a shopping spree when the new summer clothes come in.'

'Well done,' said Chris. 'You handled that very assertively.'

'I'm really proud of you,' Mark smiled. 'You've never stood up to your mother before. How do you feel?'

'Very guilty indeed, the whole time I was talking to

44

her I had butterflies in my stomach, but I kept reminding myself that I have rights too and that I don't have to please everybody. If I'd not been assertive I would have given in to her and lost the chance of having Easter in Rome.'

'I would probably have been rude to her,' said Mark, 'and then wound up feeling really guilty.'

Mark continued: 'I've never really thought about negotiating like that before. I was always brought up to the old method of taking a position and not giving way at all. Mind you, it never seemed to be a very efficient method. Have you got any more hints on negotiating Chris?'

'Yes: when we're negotiating we often believe that what *we* want is the answer; the other person thinks *theirs* is the right answer, and so we don't consider any other solution to the problem. If instead we were to find out both people's interests and then use a creative method of finding solutions – like brainstorming – it would often make reaching a workable compromise easier.'

'Brainstorming?' questioned Mark.

'Brainstorming is a way of generating ideas. What you do is think of every possible idea or solution and write it down, however silly it might seem. You just generate as many ideas as possible without criticising your own or anyone else's. Afterwards you go through them to see if any are feasible.'

'Perhaps we should do that over our summer holiday?' ventured Helen.

'Why not!' exclaimed Mark enthusiastically. 'Chris, will you be umpire?'

'Fine,' agreed Chris. 'What's the problem about holidays?'

'Well,' Helen explained, 'Mark wants to go to a resort somewhere like Spain or Italy where he can lie about on a beach. But I really fancy a holiday cottage somewhere in Britain.'

45

'Right,' said Chris, 'let's start by looking at your interests rather than your positions. Mark what is your interest?'

WELL NO ONE'S EVER COMPLAINED BEFORE . . .

'Basically I want somewhere hot and sunny where I can laze around.'

'Okay Mark. How about you Helen?'

'I really want to get away from hotels and popular resorts,' she replied, 'I'm surrounded by so many people all day, all wanting things from me. I'd just like to get away somewhere quiet.'

'Good,' said Chris. 'Now see how many ideas you can generate between you that would provide a holiday somewhere hot and sunny and at the same time get away from all the crowds and avoid a popular resort. I'll write them down for you.

Gite in France
Villa in Portugal
Cottage in Ireland
Apartment in Crete
Villa in Tuscany
Camping holiday
Apartment on remote Greek Island like Naxos
Paradores in Spain
Cycling in Holland

'That looks like a good start,' said Chris. 'All you have to do now is work through each one and decide if it really will offer you sun and a chance to get away from the crowds and you've got your workable compromise.

'I must be off now, I have some work to do before tomorrow morning. Have a good holiday in Rome.'

'Thank you,' said Mark and Helen, 'we will.'

Helen's Notebook

WORKABLE COMPROMISE

When you've made your point, as long as it doesn't undermine it, offer a compromise.

Not too early, not too late.

Listen to other person for clues.

Find out their interest, not their position.

Work with them to find a way in which both your interests can be satisfied — brainstorm ideas.

RIGHTS

* To change your mind.

47

CHAPTER FIVE

DEALING WITH CRITICISM

*In which Mark and Helen learn how to accept criticism assertively,
and Mark finds out how to deal with his difficult boss.*

*　　*　　*　　*　　*

Helen had just returned from saying goodbye to her mother
at the station . . .

'Did she catch her train all right?' asked Mark, as they
settled down for an evening's relaxation. 'Do you think she
enjoyed her stay?'

'Yes to both questions,' laughed Helen. 'I really think
she did enjoy herself and she didn't make any comments
about not having been here for Easter.

'Things are much easier between us since I started
to become more assertive. Chris is right, as *I* behave more
assertively other people are responding by being more
assertive with me. Mother seems to have picked up the
message from us that it's perfectly all right for her to ask for
what she wants. This is the first visit when she's clearly said
that she would like to do certain things. Do you remember
how she used to suggest what she thought *we* wanted to do,
rather than what she really wanted?'

'Vividly,' replied Mark, 'I'll never forget the theatre
trip last Christmas when she suggested going to the ballet
because she thought you would like it. You agreed because
you thought it was what she really wanted, when in fact
both of you wanted to see the Noel Coward play on at the
Royal Court!'

Helen smiled, 'Yes I remember that, that's something I won't do again. Since Chris appeared it's amazing how we've both changed. I'm much better now at asking for what I want. I'm gaining confidence and finding it easier to be assertive and not to put myself down. I was really pleased with myself at lunchtime when for the first time ever I complained about a meal in a restaurant.'

'Good for you,' Mark replied. 'What happened?'

'Well, mother and I went to the Old Quay for lunch, only to discover that since you and I were last there it had changed hands. They must have a different chef because the food isn't anywhere near as good as it used to be. Our meal today was absolutely appalling – the soup was lumpy and more like flour paste than soup, the meat was totally tasteless, and the vegetables were over-cooked and watery.'

'Ugh,' responded Mark, pulling a face, 'so what did you do?'

'Well, I thought carefully about whether this was the right time to be assertive and decided it was. I felt nervous about complaining but I remembered what Chris had said about breathing deeply so I took some really deep breaths which calmed me down, and then I asked to see the manager.

'When he appeared I explained that the meal was dreadful and told him about the lumpy soup and so on. He was really nice, he apologised and told me that Mother and I could have anything we wanted from the menu at no cost. I was so amazed at myself and so was Mother. Whenever anything like that happened to her I remember her either saying nothing and then moaning about it for days and days, or else, occasionally, becoming very aggressive and being rude to the waiter.'

'Like me,' admitted Mark. 'In the past I would probably have been rude to the manager. Well done Helen, you really are becoming assertive.'

'Talking about becoming more assertive,' Mark went

49

on, 'I've got a problem at work and I could do with some hints on how to deal with it assertively.'

'Oh dear,' said Helen looking concerned, what's the matter?'

'James, my new boss, is turning out to be very difficult to work for. Sometimes it seems that all he ever does is try to find fault with whatever any of us do. He even criticises my timekeeping which is normally so good, and the other day he was having a go at me for the way I spoke to one of my clerks. James thought I was much too easy-going. I feel as if I can't do anything right. It's so disheartening. If he wasn't my boss I'd really tell him what I thought of him.'

'Poor Mark,' said Helen sympathetically. 'I remember in my first teaching job I had a head teacher just like that. Every mistake I made was jumped on and I became more and more nervous and made more mistakes. I left that school with very little confidence in my work yet when I moved to another school with a different head teacher who really encouraged me and helped me to realise the skills I had, I started to develop confidence and stopped making mistakes.'

'I remember that,' said Mark. 'You hated that first school didn't you? I remember how you used to come home really upset sometimes, feeling that you couldn't do anything right.

'The question is, how do we handle the problem assertively? It seems quite different from some of the other situations Chris has described, especially as he's my boss. It's one thing being assertive with friends and strangers but another when it's someone in authority. I could do with having a talk to Chris.'

'Well,' Helen responded, 'Chris is coming round this morning so you'll be able to.'

No sooner had she spoken than the doorbell rang.

50

'That'll be Chris now,' Helen said, getting up to answer the door. She returned a moment later. 'Why don't you two have a chat while I go and make some coffee?'

Without much ado Mark started: 'Chris I have a problem at work I'd really like to talk over with you.'

'Fire away,' said Chris, settling down comfortably onto the sofa.

'As I've probably told you, I have a new boss who joined the department a couple of weeks ago. He's relatively young and hasn't been with the company long. He's under some pressure to do really well in this job and I think he's very nervous about it. He certainly doesn't seem to have too much confidence.

'Anyway, the main problem is that he's forever criticising everyone in the department. It seems as though he almost waits for us to make a mistake then pounces. He criticises the smallest thing and never says that anyone has done a job well. It's really disheartening, and morale in the department is so low at the moment it's almost non-existent.'

'I know what you mean,' agreed Chris, 'I've met people like that too. Can you give me any examples of the way he does this?'

Mark thought for a moment, 'One of the things he does is to ask me to do a piece of work which he says will only take a short time and then he complains if it takes longer. Last week he asked me to write a report for him. "Don't worry," he said, "it'll only take you an hour or two." In fact it took me the best part of two days to collect all the information and put it together.

'To make matters worse only an hour or so after asking me to write the report he was out saying "Haven't you finished that report yet?" When I finally finished the report and gave it to him all he did was point out a typing error! He even criticises me for how I handle my staff: the other day he complained because he thought I was too easy-going with one of my clerks.

'He's extremely negative and will always tell me what he doesn't like about my work, never anything he does like. I've done a lot of work on getting our financial systems onto

51

computer and all he does is point out the errors: he's never once said anything good about it. What can I do about it Chris? Are there any assertiveness techniques to deal with the problem?'

'Yes,' said Chris, 'there are some techniques to help and you've given lots of examples for us to work on.

'We haven't yet talked about dealing with criticism, which is a very difficult area for most people.

'Perhaps we could start by looking at why criticism is such a problem. How do you feel when he criticises you Mark?'

'Dreadful,' said Mark. 'My stomach turns over and I feel like a naughty child. It was the same when I had a similar boss years ago who was really aggressive and critical towards me. In fact when anyone criticises me I feel like I did as a child when my mother shouted at me for leaving my toys out.'

'Can you remember what your mother said to you?' Chris asked.

'Oh, she used to say that I was untidy, careless, thoughtless and that I didn't deserve nice toys. Even when I grew up and left home if I didn't write or ring her when she expected I was labelled as thoughtless and inconsiderate. Invariably her criticism of me was followed by her becoming really angry or not speaking to me for ages and as a child I remember sometimes being sent to bed early.'

'That's exactly why most of us find criticism so hard to take,' Chris responded. 'Most parents, instead of criticising our behaviour, tend to criticise us as people. Rather than point out that when we're in a hurry we occasionally knock things over, or that we sometimes forget to put away our toys, they say that we are lazy, stupid, clumsy, selfish or whatever.'

'So,' Mark said thoughtfully, 'you mean that when we become adults and are criticised we still feel that we are bad people and wait for the anger or silence or punishment? No wonder most people can't take criticism.

WHEN CRITICISED WE TEND TO FEEL
LIKE WE DID AS CHILDREN WHEN WE
WERE TOLD OFF...

'So how do you deal with it assertively, Chris?'

'Well, if we look at how we could respond aggressively and non-assertively to criticism that will put the assertive behaviour in context.

'First the non-assertive response is usually to say sorry and to seek forgiveness. The non-assertive person takes criticism to heart and feels that they can't do anything right. ''I'm terribly sorry I haven't finished this report yet, I'll try to work quicker, things really seem to be taking me a long time at present.''

'This doesn't really help because if you start behaving like a victim, feeling terribly sorry for yourself, you can find that the other person starts to persecute you. Responding like this also doesn't do your self-esteem any good!'

'On the other hand, the aggressive response is to defend your position and possibly even attack the other person: ''No I wasn't late finishing that report, anyway you didn't give me enough time to prepare it.'' This invariably leads to a row because the other person is likely to keep criticising you and trying to win their point.

'The assertive response is not to defend, seek forgiveness or attack the other person. You listen to what they say and if the criticism is valid you agree with it, using some of their words – this is called **negative assertion**.'

'So when my boss says that I have made a mistake in something I've done, you mean I just agree with him and say, ''Yes, I have made a mistake.'' '

'Yes,' Chris agreed, 'providing you really did make a mistake.'

'But, isn't that non-assertive?' asked Mark. 'Won't I lose and my boss win – and why shouldn't I defend myself?'

'If we defend we get into a major argument and we fuel the anger of our critic. By accepting valid criticism we tend to stop the process. It's okay to make mistakes, not to know something or not to understand, so it doesn't mean we're dreadful people if we get it wrong. By calmly accepting that

54

we aren't perfect and that we do make mistakes we don't lose any status.'

'Non-assertive behaviour is to apologise and feel really bad about it and, yes, you're right, that certainly is losing. The non-assertive person takes all criticism very personally.

'The assertive person listens to, and accepts valid criticism remembering that it is not criticism of them as a person – it is about their *behaviour*. There are also some rights that the assertive person accepts – **the right to make mistakes** and **the right not to understand something**. If they do make a mistake it's not the end of the world; they realise that they're human, not perfect.

'Is it always safe to respond to criticism assertively?' asked Mark, looking somewhat unconvinced.

'No, not always, but the assertive person will weigh up the situation and think carefully about the consequences of being assertive before they speak. The technique of negative assertion we've talked about is probably quite safe to use with anybody, but before using other assertive techniques to deal with criticism from your boss you will have to think about the effect it might have on him.'

At that moment Helen appeared from the kitchen carrying mugs of coffee.

'I heard what you said about dealing with valid criticism, but what do you do if the criticism is invalid?' she asked.

'Well, in that case you say clearly and with conviction that it is incorrect.'

'But,' Helen continued, 'I tend to think that if someone criticises me then what they say must be justified and I usually believe the criticism.'

'A lot of people do that,' Chris nodded, 'but it's important that you look at the criticism and decide for yourself whether it's valid or not. It's up to *you* to judge your behaviour, not other people.'

'Why don't we try it out,' Chris suggested. 'If both of

you could produce a list of four or five things that are valid criticisms of yourselves and four or five that are invalid, we can practise dealing with the criticism.'

*   *   *   *   *

Mark and Helen both thought for a while and then produced their lists.

'Right, who wants to be criticised first?' asked Chris.

'I suppose that as it's my problem I'd better be first,' said Mark a little warily.

'Okay Helen,' continued Chris, 'what you do is to make a valid criticism of Mark and then an invalid one and work your way down the lists. Mark, you have to remember not to justify, defend, apologise or verbally attack Helen, just agree, using some of Helen's words, if it's valid, and disagree if it's invalid.'

'Mark, you can be very untidy sometimes.'

'You're right Helen: I can be very untidy sometimes.'

'You're not a very good cook.'

'That's completely untrue Helen: I'm a very good cook.'

'You're impatient when things go wrong.'

'That's right, I do get impatient when things go wrong.'

'Mark, you're hopeless at remembering anniversaries and birthdays.'

'That's totally wrong: I'm particularly good at remembering anniversaries and birthdays.'

'Well done,' said Chris. 'Now it's your turn Mark.'

'Helen, you're very indecisive sometimes.'

'Yes Mark, I am very indecisive sometimes.'

'You're a very untidy cook.'

'That's not true Mark, I'm a very tidy cook.'

'You panic so easily.'

'Yes I do panic easily, I do tend to let problems get on top of me.'

'That's amazing,' said Mark sounding surprised. 'Being criticised was nowhere near as bad as I'd imagined.

Normally, I would have defended myself and said no I'm not untidy, or rounded on Helen reminding her that she's untidy too, and then we would have ended up having a row.

'This way I felt in control yet could accept the criticism. I thought it would feel as if Helen had won and I'd lost, but it didn't, I felt okay. When I was criticising Helen I felt as if she was in control too.'

'How about you Helen?' Chris asked.

'Normally, as Mark says, he defends himself and I then get so angry because I feel that he's not really listening to me. This time it seemed as though he was listening to me and then he was deciding whether or not he would accept the criticism.

'When he criticised me that was very different, because normally I would have felt dreadful and would have apologised profusely. But somehow agreeing with the criticism without apologising helped me to keep my self-esteem. The whole time we were criticising each other it felt as though we were equals.'

'That's the whole point of this way of dealing with criticism,' Chris responded. 'The person being criticised doesn't lose any status and both people can feel equal, rather than criticism feeling like a battlefield with victors and vanquished.'

'Okay,' said Mark. 'You've told us what to do if the criticism is totally valid or totally invalid, but what if it is only partly correct like the other morning when the boss criticised me for being late and the way he talked about it you would have thought that I was never on time?'

'If only a bit of it is justified it's basically the same technique. You acknowledge the part that is correct but you can refute what isn't – "You're late as usual." "Yes I was late this morning but normally I'm early."

'Let's have another go – try something which is only partly valid Helen.'

'Mark, you can be very aggressive.'

57

'Yes,' agreed Mark, 'I can be very aggressive some-times, but not always, and it's an area I'm working on and improving.'

'That's good. Look, we've covered a lot of ground this time, without even fully dealing with your problem Mark. Handling criticism is a big area and one that is very difficult for most people. Why don't we stop there for today and let you practise criticising each other and dealing with that assertively. We could get together again soon and I'll finish telling you the other techniques to help with criticism – both receiving and giving it.'

'That's fine by us,' said Mark. Helen nodded. 'You have covered a lot of ground; I don't think I could take in too much more today.'

'Why don't you come up to the Coach and Horses one evening for a meal?' asked Chris. 'My treat.'

'That would be nice,' Helen responded enthusiastical-ly, 'we haven't been there for ages. Don't they do barbeques at this time of year if the weather's good?'

'Yes, they do,' Chris answered. 'How about meeting up there on Friday evening at about seven?'

'We'll look forward to it,' said Mark and Helen.

'By the way,' said Chris, 'how did you two get on with coming to a workable compromise about your summer holiday?'

'Fine,' said Mark. 'We thought about all the ideas we'd brainstormed and finally decided to have an apartment in Tuscany because we thought that it would be hot and sunny for me, yet away from all the holiday crowds for Helen. We're going at the beginning of September.'

'That sounds ideal,' Chris replied with a smile. 'I hope you have a really good time.'

Helen's notebook

DEALING WITH CRITICISM

Don't defend, seek forgiveness or attack the other person.

Consider the criticism and decide whether it's valid or not. Just because someone has made a criticism doesn't mean that it's correct!

NEGATIVE ASSERTION

If the criticism is valid, agree with it, using some of the critic's words.
" Yes you're quite right, I was late this morning."

If the criticism is invalid say so.

RIGHTS

*   To make a mistake.

*   Not to understand something.

59

CHAPTER SIX

MORE ON CRITICISM

In which Mark and Helen learn how to deal with put-downs, and discover how to give criticism.

* * * * *

The following Friday Mark and Helen met Chris at the Coach and Horses as arranged. The three of them sat outside in the evening sunshine . . .

'How have you been getting on with criticism since I last saw you?' Chris asked.

Mark started, 'Very well really. I'm beginning to learn to cope with valid criticism. The other day James was absolutely furious because I'd not done something I should have done. I just said "You're quite right I should have done that." It completely took the wind out of his sails. He didn't say another word.

'I also had a chance to do something about his smoke-screening yesterday. James came into my office to ask me to do another report for him which he said would only take me a couple of hours. Instead of just accepting this, I asked him what the report involved, what information I would need to collect, and when he needed it. I also explained that I was busy for the rest of the day but could start work on it tomorrow. It took a bit of effort on my part to find out exactly what it involved and how long it would take but eventually he agreed that it was a few days work not a couple of hours.'

'In my case,' said Helen, 'I've been learning to stop

saying sorry every time I'm criticised, but to look at the criticism and decide if it's valid or not. If it is valid I accept it and remember that I'm not perfect, it's okay to make mistakes and a criticism about what I do is not a criticism about me as a person.

'I'm realising how much I used to accept that any criticism of me was automatically valid, I never really questioned it – if someone said it, it must be justified. When I was young my mother often used to criticise my clothes so I always assumed that my dress sense was not very good. After we spoke to you I started to question that along with some other beliefs I had and realised that in fact she was wrong!'

'We're also finding,' Mark continued, 'that it's becoming easier for us to criticise each other. Before, if Helen was the slightest bit critical of me I used to get really angry. Now I'm beginning to learn to accept criticism. Criticisms of each other aren't now necessarily developing into rows the way they would have done before.'

'That's really good,' Chris smiled. 'You're obviously getting on all right with negative assertion, so, as I promised, I have some more techniques to help you.

'We've looked at straightforward criticism, but we've not yet talked about put-downs, which may or may not be valid. Put-downs can be used to manipulate you into doing something you don't want to, to try to make you feel guilty or inadequate in some way or they may be just plain nagging.'

'You mean like my boss asking if I'd finished the report yet?'

'Absolutely,' Chris agreed. 'That certainly is a put-down, intended no doubt to make you feel that you can't do your job properly. Put-downs can be dealt with using a technique called **fogging**.

'When someone puts you down they need some reaction from you, something they can hook on to and criticise more. Fogging prevents this because you accept the partial

61

truth, the logic or even the possibility of the truth in what they say, without confirming whether the criticism is valid or not.

'You say things like: "I can understand why you think that", "That's a good point", "Yes I am sometimes late", "That could be true". You're not offering them any resistance and this tends to stop them putting you down.'

'So,' Chris continued, 'if they say, "I can't find this report: you really must be careful when you're filing them or one could get lost," your reply could be, "That's absolutely right: if I don't file them carefully one could get lost."

'I think I understand,' said Mark tentatively. 'So, when my boss starts nagging me for being slow with a report I could reply, "I can understand you thinking that I'm slow at times." '

'Yes, that's fogging,' said Chris, 'and if you do that you should eventually stop the put-downs and open up channels for straight communication.'

'There's another technique which will also help you with your boss. It's called **negative enquiry**. This is a way of asking for more information about whatever it is you're being criticised about. So, if someone at work accuses you of being careless in presenting your reports, you would ask for more information – "In what way do you see my reports as being carelessly presented?" That way you'll find out whether it *is* a major problem or something as minor as a single typing mistake.

'You can use negative enquiry with negative assertion, so if your boss says, "You were too easy-going with that clerk," you could reply, "Yes I was easy-going. Do you think I could have been firmer?" '

'And', interrupted Mark, 'if I used that technique when my boss went on about me being slow with the report I suppose I could have said, "Yes, this report *is* taking me some time. Are you anxious about that?" '

'Yes you could,' nodded Chris. 'Why don't you try out an example with Helen?'

'Yes, why not,' he agreed. 'We could use some more examples from our lists. Okay Helen, try criticising me.'

'Right,' said Helen. 'I really feel unhappy about the way you leave things to the last minute.'

'Yes I do leave things to the last minute. How does this affect you?'

'I get very frustrated when we end up doing all our important jobs in a short time and things get forgotten or left out.'

'What particular things get left to the last minute and forgotten?'

'Well, last week we had some important letters to write that ended up being put off for a couple of days.'

'Okay,' Chris interrupted, 'before you get too involved in it. How did that feel Mark?'

'Very good, because instead of getting angry at what I assumed Helen was criticising me for, as I would have done in the past, I was able to find out exactly what the problem was.'

'Fine. How about you Helen?'

'The main thing for me was that it made me think about what the problem really was and not just moan about Mark putting things off.'

'So, you've seen one way of using negative enquiry. It can enable you to find out exactly what the problem is and whether it is something you do all the time or just occasionally.

'Also, as well as asking for information about any of your mistakes, you can ask for positive information. I first did this at a meeting where some work I had done came under heavy criticism from a colleague. When he had finished with all the negative comments I simply asked him what he liked about it. His attitude changed as he talked enthusiastically about all the positive things. If I hadn't asked, though, I would only have heard the negatives.'

'So I suppose I could use this with my boss when he's being negative, as he was over the report?'

63

'Yes,' said Chris, 'you could use negative assertion to accept any mistakes you've made, and then ask for positive feedback on what he did like. Equally, you could use it next time he criticises your work with the computer systems.'

'One of the other advantages of negative enquiry,' Chris continued, 'is that if your critic is not genuine but is trying to manipulate you or put you down, negative enquiry will show this up because the manipulator is not likely to have, or want to give you, specific information on what you've done wrong. They may well just be rude or avoid answering you.'

'We used to have a lecturer at college like that,' chipped in Helen. 'He used to say things like, "You'll have difficulties with this . . . " If any of the students questioned him as to what he meant he just avoided answering them or said something like "Well if you don't know by now . . . " '

'You've told us a lot about receiving criticism, Chris,' said Mark, 'but what about giving it? I have a number of trainee accountants and clerks working under me and I have to give them feedback about their work and how they're progressing.'

Chris nodded, 'There are a number of guidelines you can follow when giving criticism to others. One of the most important things to remember is not to give only negative criticism about things people have done badly, but also to give them positive comments about what they've done well. As you've discovered, Mark, being given the negative side only is very demoralising and you start to wonder if you've done anything right at all.

'People need praise and compliments as much as negative criticism in order to develop and learn. Remember how we encourage a child to walk. When it takes its first tottering steps we don't complain that it isn't doing it properly, we praise it for what it *can* do. Yet we often tend to forget that fact when dealing with older children and adults.

'Another useful guideline is to be specific – it's much

64

more helpful to say, "The way you wrote out that information made it really easy for me to read. I particularly liked the subheadings," than to say "That was a great piece of work."

'We've talked before about describing behaviour rather than criticising the person. It's also helpful if you *own* the criticism by saying 'I think . . . ", "I feel . . . ", rather than "You are . . . ". It's better to say, "I feel angry when you leave your school books in the sitting room," which describes behaviour, rather than, "You're really untidy the way you leave your school books around," which is a judgement about the person.

'Once we've started to criticise someone, we often remember lots of other things we would also like to criticise but this will invariably confuse the issue, so resist the temptation and stick to the point.

'Last but not least, think what giving the criticism is saying about you, the critic. The criticism we give others says a lot about ourselves and our values and sometimes we see our own faults mirrored in others.'

'That's really helpful Chris,' said Helen, 'I shall put that into practice when I'm teaching. I'm now feeling much happier about giving and receiving criticism, and I've always felt happy about giving people compliments, but what about receiving compliments? I tend to get quite embarrassed when people compliment me – I never know what to say.'

'Yes, I know what you mean,' said Chris. 'When receiving compliments many of us do the same as we do with criticism – we argue with them. When complimented on something we have done we say, "Oh it was nothing really," or when someone says how good we look we laugh it off or say something like, "Who me?" or we throw the compliment back at the other person. If they say, "That's a nice outfit you're wearing," we reply, "Yours is nice too." What we're really saying is no thank you to the compliment.

65

WHEN GIVING CRITICISM THINK WHAT IT SAYS ABOUT YOU THE CRITIC . . .

'The assertive response is to acknowledge the compliment: "Thank you, it's nice to be appreciated," "I'm glad you like this outfit." Or "It's reassuring that you think this colour suits me; I wasn't too sure," Or to agree with it: "Thank you, this dress is a favourite of mine too."'

'Thank you Chris, I really appreciate the time and trouble you've taken to teach us about dealing with criticism.'

'Thank you Helen, I'm glad you're finding it so useful,' said Chris with a smile.

Helen's Notebook

FOGGING

* Stops put-downs and manipulative criticism.

* Agree with the partial truth, logic or possibility of truth in the criticism without confirming whether criticism is valid or not –
'I can understand you thinking that.'
'That's a good point.'

NEGATIVE ENQUIRY

* Asking for information on what you're being criticised about.

* Can be used with negative assertion.
'Yes I am non-assertive. How does this affect you?'

* Also use to ask for positive information when it's not forthcoming.

GIVING CRITICISM - GUIDELINES

* Give positives too. * Be specific.
* Describe behaviour; don't judge the person.
* Own the criticism. * Stick to the point.
* Think what it says about you the critic.

CHAPTER SEVEN

RELATIONSHIPS

In which Mark and Helen discover how to use assertiveness to deal with anger and grudges and to improve close relationships.

*   *   *   *   *

Mark and Helen had recently returned from their holiday in Tuscany and were lazing in the garden enjoying some late afternoon summer sunshine . . .

'I did enjoy our holiday,' said Helen. 'That apartment in Tuscany was idyllic, I'd like to go back there again one day. I'm glad Chris introduced us to the art of negotiating assertively and finding a workable compromise.'

'Yes,' said Mark, 'I'm amazed at all the changes that have happened to us and our life together since Chris started to teach us about assertiveness.'

'Mmm,' Helen murmured lazily, 'and I'm delighted at the way things have improved for me now that I'm able to ask for what I want. What surprises me though is how quickly some of the changes have happened. Like yesterday when I said to you that I needed to have an evening off and just watch a video. Only a short time ago I would have skirted round what I wanted, just hinting at it.'

'Yes,' replied Mark, 'I was so pleased last week, when you *told* me what you wanted to do for your birthday. If you hadn't said that you would like to go to the theatre for a change, I would have booked a table for dinner in our usual restaurant thinking that was what you most wanted.'

'And I', replied Helen, 'would have gone along for

69

dinner thinking that if that was where you wanted to take me then it would be ungrateful of me to suggest something else.' They both laughed.

'By the way, how's James been since we've been back from holiday?' she asked.

'Much better,' Mark replied. 'As you know, just before we went away, he was being particularly critical and after I'd accepted anything he said that was valid, I asked if I could have some positive comments as well as the negative ones. Well, he's really taken this to heart and has been at pains to point out the good work that we're all doing. Our relationship is much better now and morale in the department has improved dramatically.'

'Oh good, I am pleased,' Helen smiled. 'We've learnt a lot about assertiveness, but I wonder if there are other ways we could use it in our relationship.'

'Yes,' Mark mused, 'there must be more that we could learn about. It would be nice to talk to Chris about it.'

At that moment the phone rang. Mark went to answer it, returning several minutes later.

'Would you believe that was Chris ringing to ask how we enjoyed Tuscany and how things were going with my boss. I explained what I've just told you and went on to say what you and I had been discussing and Chris has offered to pop round to talk it over.'

'Oh good,' replied Helen. 'It'll be nice to see Chris again, it's ages since we last met. I'll go and make some fresh lemonade.'

A short while later Chris appeared and settled down in the garden with Mark and Helen.

'How was the holiday?' began Chris.

'Absolutely lovely,' replied Helen, 'the weather was glorious and Mark was able to laze about and relax in the sun. We had a delightful apartment – a converted farmhouse right in the middle of the most beautiful countryside. We were well away from the crowds so I got the peace and quiet I needed. Although we did have a few days away from the peace of the country visiting Florence, which was wonderful. All in all it was exactly what we both wanted.'

'Good, I am glad,' said Chris. 'Okay, so what can I do to help you more with assertiveness?'

'Well,' Helen started, 'as Mark has said to you, we were talking about how learning to be assertive has had an effect on our relationship. Although the problems we've talked to you about have been with people at work, friends, strangers and my mother, we've also applied some of the techniques to our lives together and found them very helpful.'

'In particular,' Mark took up the story, 'Helen can now ask for what she wants and both of us are learning to accept criticism from each other. We were delighted with the workable compromise over our holiday and we wondered if there were other ways we could use assertive behaviour in our relationship?'

'Have you any particular problems that you would like to look at?' asked Chris.

Mark and Helen thought for a few moments.

'Yes,' said Helen, 'we do seem to get into rows that I wish we could prevent.'

'Yes, I'd go along with that,' said Mark. 'That is certainly one of our major problems.'

'Okay,' said Chris, 'how do the rows start?'

'It's nearly always the same,' said Helen. 'I get annoyed at something Mark does, which is usually something quite minor. I tend to feel that I can't say anything about it at the time so I sit on my anger and then eventually, over maybe days or weeks these small things build up so much that I blow my top and we have a row. It feels a bit like being a volcano with the pressure building up with each irritation until I erupt.'

'The same goes for me,' said Mark, and the little irritations don't even have to be things that Helen has done, they could be happening at work and then when I come home Helen says something and that's the final straw – I explode.'

71

'I know what you mean,' said Chris with feeling. 'We bear grudges against the other person and collect them until one day we let them all out in a major row, or we snipe and just get at the other person without saying clearly what the problem is. Neither way is ideal. However, there are assertive ways to deal with grudges and irritations.

'The first thing you need to do is to deal with your feelings of anger because if you are extremely angry then you won't be able to deal with the problem assertively.

'When I find myself getting angry I find it very helpful to think about whether I have a genuine grievance or whether it's something in my upbringing that says I should be annoyed.'

'What do you mean?' asked Mark, looking puzzled.

'Well, when we're hurt, angry or upset by something that has happened we often make the original feelings much worse than they would have been by what we say to ourselves about it – our "self-talk". We say things to ourselves like, "If they were really a good friend they would have helped me." Or, "If they really liked the present I sent they would have thanked me immediately." And by doing this we can really wind ourselves up.'

'I know what you mean,' Helen interrupted. 'This year for the first time ever Mark forgot our wedding anniversary. There was no present or card and he only realised it was our anniversary when I gave him his present.

'At the time I felt rather sad but a couple of hours later I had really wound myself up by saying to myself that he didn't care any more; if he really loved me he would have remembered. Foolishly I mentioned it to Mother and she didn't help either, saying how awful he was to forget it. By the end of the morning I was *so* angry.'

'And what about your problem with table knives?' Mark laughed. Chris looked puzzled.

Helen explained: 'My mother always taught me to hold my table knife a certain way and until I was in my mid-twenties I really used to think that there was something wrong with people who held their knives differently. It took me years to convince myself that in fact it doesn't matter a bit how you hold it.'

'That's just what I mean,' Chris replied. 'The problem is that we tend to think that our way of living and of viewing the world is *the* way and if people do things differently we think they're bad or inferior.

'One way of dealing with this is to reverse the self-talk and to look at the reality of the situation. If a friend says no to us and we start telling ourselves that they can't really be a good friend, we can challenge the self-talk. Why can't they be a good friend and still say no to us? If someone forgets a birthday or anniversary we can challenge any thoughts we have about them not really caring about us.

'It also helps to imagine yourself in the other person's shoes to see things from their point of view. I can't always do that on the same day that I feel angry; I usually have to calm down first. But invariably if I look at the situation from the other person's point of view, I realise that in the same situation I may well have done the same thing. Even if I realise that I would have behaved differently, I usually find that at least I have much more understanding of why they behaved as they did.'

'Doesn't that mean that you repress your emotions?' asked Mark.

'No it doesn't,' Chris replied. 'Repressing emotions is very dangerous and is like Helen's description of the volcano – sometime or other they're going to erupt. No, by doing this you don't repress anything, you just look at the situation realistically and see if your self-talk has made the situation worse.'

'What do you do about the feeling of anger itself?' asked Mark. 'I find that if I get angry there is so much emotion in me that I have to let off steam before I can even think sensibly.'

'You're right Mark: if you're that angry you usually need to deal with the anger first and there are lots of ways

73

of doing that such as playing sport, hitting a punch ball, crying, punching a pillow or cushion, sitting in your car alone with the windows closed and shouting your head off, or writing to the person you're feeling angry with but not posting the letter.

'The assertive way of dealing with grudges and irritations is not to let the pressure build up too much, but to tackle the irritations as they arise.

'If you work on challenging your self-talk, put yourself in the other person's place and if necessary let off steam, then you should be calm enough to express your anger to the other person assertively.'

'If you're expressing anger, isn't that going to be aggressive?' asked Mark.

'Not necessarily,' replied Chris. 'You can tell someone you're angry in a way that is assertive rather than aggressive. As ever, the first thing in assertive behaviour is to work out what you want from the situation and whether that is realistic. If you have felt hurt you may want the other person to grovel, but that's not realistic. All you may achieve is a chance to express your feelings, or on the other hand the other person may go as far as deciding to change their behaviour as a result of what you've said.

'When you do talk to them, choose your time and place carefully and then tell them what has upset you, using the techniques of giving criticism that we talked about last time. Don't be aggressive, don't blame them but tell them how angry, hurt, upset or whatever you feel. Be careful not to be sarcastic or to become aggressive.

'I first practised this with a friend who used to come round to see me and would settle down and then talk for hours and hours about herself and what she'd been doing. She never asked me about what I'd been doing or even asked my opinion about what she was saying. It wasn't a conversation – I was talked at.

'After one particular day when she'd talked non-stop about her life for about four or five hours, I was so angry that

KNOWING WHAT YOU
WANT IS THE FIRST STEP
IN ASSERTIVENESS..

I decided to do something about it. I went through all the techniques we've just talked about. I wrote a letter, which helped me let off steam, even though I had no intention of posting it. I looked at whether I had talked myself into getting more angry than necessary – I realised that I had been saying to myself that she thought nothing of me or she would ask about me, she didn't care about *my* thoughts or opinions, all she wanted was someone to listen to her. I was able to challenge most of that self-talk.

'I then considered how I would feel in my friend's situation – living alone with few people to talk to, and eventually I reduced my anger to a manageable level.

'When I'd calmed down, the next time I saw her I was able to say to her assertively exactly how I felt, that I felt belittled when she didn't ask about my life or ask for any contribution from me in the conversation.

'Once I had expressed how I felt she looked quite shocked and said that she hadn't realised that she was doing that at all. She asked me to point out if she started to do it again and since then things have considerably improved. We now have proper conversations.'

'Perhaps I should try this on Mother,' suggested Helen. 'She has a habit of talking non-stop and not including me.'

'If we're going to tell each other when something has upset us,' Mark said slowly, 'then I presume we're going to be thinking of changing our behaviour.'

'Yes,' Chris agreed, 'when you've talked over the things that irritate you, both of you may recognise the need for a change in your behaviour.'

'But couldn't we become like James at work, constantly complaining?'

'You could,' said Chris dryly, 'or you could use more positive ways of helping each other to change. Rather than criticising what you don't like, you could concentrate on the good things, asking each other to increase those.'

'You mean like saying I'd like Mark to be tidier

rather than saying I'd like him to stop being untidy.'

'Exactly,' said Chris. 'It's amazing what a difference it makes when instead of criticising someone for not coming up to scratch, you compliment them for doing things well. We often do things because we are afraid that if we don't, our partners will be angry. But if we can do things because it will please the other person, rather than out of fear, this does tend to make a considerable difference to our relationship, putting it onto a more positive footing.

'Remember though, when deciding on change, to make sure that you're *both* working on things – otherwise one person may feel they're the only one!'

'Thank you, those ideas sound really helpful Chris,' said Helen enthusiastically. 'We'll let you know how we get on.

'By the way, Chris, while you're here, there *is* one other thing I'd like to ask you about.'

'Fire away,' said Chris.

'Well, over the past couple of years I've been for a number of interviews for jobs as a deputy head teacher, but with no luck so far. There's a possibility that another job for a deputy head will be coming up in the near future. It's in a school not far from here and it's a job that I'd really like.

'I have a feeling that I haven't been successful before because of my non-assertiveness and I would like to look at how I can stop *this* job slipping through my fingers.

'I'm realising that assertiveness isn't *just* a question of using techniques like fielding; it's a way of approaching life, and I'd like to know more about how I could take an assertive approach to applying for this job.'

'Fine,' said Chris, 'then perhaps we should start by considering why you haven't been successful before. Have you any ideas Helen?'

'Mm,' murmured Helen, looking thoughtful, 'I'm not sure that I was ready for the position of deputy head when I applied for the previous jobs. I suppose that although I

77

ASSERTIVENESS IS A WAY OF APPROACHING LIFE,
NOT JUST A QUESTION OF TECHNIQUES...

did know that I wanted the post, it may not have been realistic. Certainly, at the time of my last interview, which was for a deputy head's job in my own school, I hadn't had enough management experience within the school and I was relying on the hope that as I'd been quietly getting on doing my job well, my efforts would be recognised and I'd be promoted.'

'A lot of people tend to believe that,' Chris replied, 'but in fact, as well as doing your present job well, you do need to bring yourself to the attention of senior staff and to make it known that you're interested in promotion. The problem is that people tend to take us at face value. If we quietly get on with our job and don't mention that we want promotion we may be labelled as someone who likes the job they're already in and doesn't want to get on.

'How did you feel about getting promoted? Did you think you'd be successful?'

'No, not really I suppose,' Helen answered. 'I've always had a feeling of being somehow unworthy, a "Who me? I couldn't do that" feeling. I suppose that if I felt that then my body language and tone of voice would give me away in the interview, even if the words I said implied that I wanted the job.'

'Yes,' Chris replied, 'they would certainly give you away. And if you put yourself down, as many people do because they're brought up to be "modest", people will believe what you say. If I said that I only knew a little about assertiveness and I wasn't very good at it would you have any faith in me?'

'No I wouldn't, you're right Chris, so what do I do about preparing myself for this job.'

'What have you done so far Helen?'

'Nothing really,' Helen replied, 'until I learned to say no I was so busy doing what everyone asked me to do, and generally trying to please people, that I never had time to consider my own needs.'

'Well,' Chris said, 'now that you can say no, and have

some more time, one of the first things you can do is to look at your own job and decide if you're doing that in the most efficient way possible and to add any more skills that would improve your work. Then look at the job you want and decide what you could do to prepare for that one.'

'Okay,' said Helen, 'I suppose at my present teaching level I could improve some of my skills. I've specialised in music for years but my art could certainly be improved. I could do some courses in art and needlework.'

'Fine,' said Chris. 'What about the next level? What does the job entail?'

'As a deputy head there'd be a considerable amount of administration and management, so any training courses in management, planning, administration and team-building would be very useful. I could even do some applied psychology like Transactional Analysis to increase my interpersonal skills.'

'How about an assertiveness course?' asked Chris with a smile.

'I suppose that's one course I can't miss out,' Helen laughed. 'I won't find all of these run as in-service courses but I assume that I can find evening classes or weekend courses at a college.'

'You're right,' Chris responded, 'I did my first weekend assertiveness course at the local university.'

'You also mentioned before about getting myself noticed,' Helen continued. 'What do you mean exactly?'

'Well,' Chris replied, 'you could make sure that when you attend meetings you contribute to them. Some people are so intimidated by meetings that they never speak. You could also take on some extra jobs such as heading a working party, anything that will bring you to people's attention. Even if you're not applying for a job in your own school someone there will be writing a reference for you.'

80

'The other thing you need to address is your own self-esteem, this "Who me?" feeling.'

'I agree Chris, I've had problems since I was a small

child. I've always considered myself an also-ran, but since I started to learn about assertiveness my self-esteem has improved considerably, although I still feel I could improve it more.'

Chris nodded: 'One, way you can help this is to be aware of what's going on in your head when you feel like an also-ran. Does it remind you of a time when you were younger? You may need to challenge the words you hear in your head and remind yourself of times when you were successful, to change your "Who me?" to "Yes me".

'I used to have the same problem. Whenever I got into a situation like the one you're in I could hear my mother saying, "I don't expect you to do brilliantly in the interview, or exam as long as you try your hardest," and so I believed that I wouldn't do brilliantly. Now I talk to myself and say I won't try to do my best, I will actually achieve what it is that I want. Whenever I heard the voice saying "Who me?" I learnt to replace it with "Why not me?" and to recognise that I had as many skills or qualifications as the other people. If I didn't, I went out and got them.

'High self-esteem also means accepting yourself warts and all. You don't have to be perfect so don't put yourself down if you're not.' Chris continued: 'There's one other thing you can do to build your self-esteem, and that's to treat yourself like someone very special. Give yourself presents – a bunch of flowers, a glass of good wine, a long laze in the bath with a good book, a walk in the country. It will do wonders for your self-esteem and after all if you don't treat yourself well, why should you expect others to treat you well?

'Finally – be confident. Thinking positively encourages positive things to happen.'

Helen's notebook

GRUDGES

Deal with them as they arise; don't let them build up.

DEALING WITH ANGER

Listen to your self-talk; is it making things worse?

Confront the self-talk. Remember your way of living isn't the only way.

Imagine yourself in the other person's shoes and see things from their point of view.

Discharge any anger by punching a cushion, crying, writing an unposted letter, etc.

Tell the other person calmly how you feel. Don't blame them

PREPARING FOR AN INTERVIEW

Check that you really want the job and that it's realistic to go for it.

Make sure people know you want promotion. Keep a high profile.

Build your self-esteem.

Improve skills and knowledge for your present job.

Work out what skills/knowledge you need for the new job and gain them.

CHAPTER EIGHT

THE INTERVIEW

In which Chris helps Helen with a job application, and Helen learns how to be assertive in an interview.

*　*　*　*　*

A couple of months later . . .

Helen and Mark had just returned from work and were relaxing before preparing supper.

'Mark,' said Helen excitedly, that deputy head's job has just been advertised at last, and I've definitely decided that I want to apply.'

'Good, I'm glad,' said Mark, 'and this time with all the preparation you've done you should stand a very good chance of getting the job.'

'I certainly hope so,' Helen replied. 'I'm a lot more confident this time, than I've ever been before over applying for a job. I'm so glad I talked to Chris about the job because all the courses I've done have been really useful.

'I'd better get my CV out and do some work on it, not something I'm looking forward to – I'm never sure of the best way to describe my experience, I do find it difficult to say that I'm good at something – I'm always afraid that it will sound boastful. I could really do with talking this through with Chris. Anyway let's get something to eat and then I can start work on it.'

But, before Mark and Helen could reach the kitchen the phone rang. Helen went to answer it. A few minutes later she joined Mark in the kitchen.

'That was Chris asking if I'd seen the advert for the deputy head's job and wondering if I was going to apply. I said I was, and that I would appreciate a bit of help with my CV. Chris offered to chat it over so I suggested that we have supper together here.'

'Fine,' said Mark. 'It's a while since we saw Chris – it'll be nice to get together again.'

An hour or so later Chris arrived and they settled down to eat. Over supper Chris asked Helen how she had been getting on with her courses.

'Since I last saw you', Helen explained, 'I've been on quite a lot of courses. I've done some of the evening courses designed for teachers, the local authority school managerial course, and some very interesting weekend courses, including one on assertiveness which Mark and I did together.'

'It sounds like you've been really busy,' said Chris. 'How did you enjoy the assertiveness course?'

'It was very good indeed,' Helen replied. 'I liked the way we got the chance to practise all the various techniques in a safe environment. I learned a lot by listening to all the other course members too. I thought that I used to be really non-assertive but there were people there far more non-assertive than me.'

'We did quite a bit of work on video,' Mark added. 'I found that extremely useful because I was able to watch my own body language. I also became aware of how I say things – I was amazed to see how patronising I could be.'

'That all sounds as if it's been really helpful,' Chris answered. 'Have you found that the courses have helped your self-esteem Helen?'

'Very much so,' Helen replied, 'especially the assertiveness and management courses. One of the things I liked was that they didn't just teach me new skills, but also helped me to realise all the skills I already had. That did wonders for my self-esteem. I've also been following your advice and treating myself as a special person and that has helped.'

'As a result of the assertiveness course,' she continued,

84

'I've been going along to a weekly assertiveness group, which is particularly useful because we're able to give each other the support which I find so necessary to help me change my behaviour and become more assertive.'

'Great,' said Chris, 'so what would you like me to help you with now?'

'At the moment I'm a bit concerned about my CV. I never know how much information to put in them and I'm never sure how to phrase my experience so that I do myself justice. I was brought up to be modest and I have great difficulty saying that I'm good at something. Have you any helpful hints Chris?'

'I know what you mean,' said Chris, 'and yes I do have some helpful hints. I think that the first thing when planning a CV is to find out as much as you can about the job you're applying for. Work out what skills you'll need in the job and make a list of them. Then think back through all your experience, both within and outside teaching and list all those that may be relevant.

'When it comes to describing these experiences I always tend to describe the responsibilities of the job and then explain exactly what I did and what experience I gained from it.'

'Can you give me an example of what you mean?' Helen asked.

'Yes,' said Chris: 'I know you're a youth leader, so, in describing this work you would say what the responsibilities of a youth leader are such as offering counselling, administration, arranging club events and keeping accounts. You can then describe what you've done.'

'Like organising a trip to France last year?' interrupted Helen.

'Absolutely,' Chris replied. 'Also, don't forget to describe what you've gained from the work.'

85

'You mean like saying that I gained experience in

administration and management skills, experience in dealing with an older age group and development of my own interpersonal skills?' Helen added.

'That's it,' Chris nodded.

'So, by describing what I've done, and what I've learned from it, I'm saying that I'm an experienced manager, without sounding boastful. Okay, let me see if I can think of another example.'

Helen thought for a moment. 'Right, for the past two years I've taken responsibility for music in the school. This has meant me co-ordinating the work of other teachers in this field, and organising events such as the Nativity play and carol concert. As a result I've gained considerable experience of planning and organisation, administrative and management work.'

'Fine,' said Chris, 'and don't forget that you can describe courses in the same way, stating what you gained from the course.'

'That's really helpful,' said Helen. 'Thank you Chris. I feel a lot more confident about it now.'

'Good luck,' Chris smiled. 'Let me know how you get on. If you want any help preparing an assertive approach to being interviewed, let me know.'

* * * * *

A few weeks later Helen received a letter inviting her for interview the following week . . .

Chris, who as if by magic, always seemed to know when Mark or Helen needed advice, dropped in unexpectedly one evening and agreed to stay and chat about the forthcoming interview . . .

* * * * *

'What I'm interested in', said Helen, 'is what you meant by me taking an assertive approach to being interviewed.'

'Well,' Chris responded, 'there are a number of aspects to being interviewed that can be handled assertively. You could be criticised or complimented in the interview and might wish to respond assertively. You might need to show in some of your answers that your approach to the job and problems that may arise, would, where appropriate, be assertive.

'You'll need to be able to state assertively what strengths you can bring to the job, and you may also be asked about your weaknesses. It's important to be able to describe these without putting yourself down.

'You can also follow some of the techniques we talked about when you were taking the toaster back, such as running the interview through in your mind, thinking through what they might ask you and mentally practising your answers.'

'And', chipped in Helen, 'I should know what I want to say and say it clearly and concisely without rambling.'

'Absolutely,' said Chris. 'Why don't we have a practice?'

'That *would* help,' said Helen. 'I've given some thought to what I might be asked, so it would be very useful to have a chance to practise some answers now.'

'Okay Helen. Looking at your CV it seems that until fairly recently you haven't had much management or administrative experience at school.'

'That's correct. Until recently I hadn't had a great deal of management experience within the school, but in recent years I've rather made up for that. For two years now I've been responsible for music within the school, which has involved me in co-ordinating the work of other teachers as well as organising the Nativity play and all the school's musical events.

'Recently, I've also headed a working party on curriculum development which has meant me taking on a management role co-ordinating other members of the working party.

'Although my management experience within school

has only been gained over the past two years, outside school I have had some ten years experience of management and administration as a youth leader.'

'Can you tell me something about that Helen?'

'Yes, it's involved me in quite a varied range of management tasks really, as well as offering counselling and generally helping to motivate our young people. I organise some of the club events – for example, last year I set up a trip to France – and I also do a lot of administrative jobs like keeping accounts. So really the work has not only developed my interpersonal skills but also given me lots of experience in basic administration and organisation.'

'How have you prepared yourself for this post in terms of managerial skills?'

'In addition to the experiences I've described, I've also been on a number of courses to develop my management and team-building skills, including a course in assertiveness. I've been on the local authority's school managerial course, which improved my ability to organise and plan. I've also done a number of evening classes to further my teaching skills, in dyslexia, language development for the younger age range, and art.'

'Fine, you've had a lot of experience as a classroom teacher. What do you consider to be your strengths?'

Helen thought for a moment. 'My enthusiasm as a teacher is certainly one of my strengths. Because of this I find that I can give confidence to the children. I like to feel that at the end of my year with them they value themselves more and are more capable both personally and in their work.'

'Can you tell me something about your teaching style?'

'Yes, I think my style is fairly structured and I consider myself organised and well-planned. I tend to have different children doing different things within the class, say one group working on language development with me, another group doing some work with a teaching assistant and others working on their own, practising handwriting, comprehension or working with numbers.'

89

'Some people might consider that too informal, rather than structured.'

'Yes, it's true some people might consider my style too informal, but I find that the method works well for me.'

'What would you do if a child's parents came in to complain that they weren't happy about the way you were teaching, that they expected their child to be taught rather than to work on their own?'

'That's quite a difficult question; I'd like to take a minute or two to think about it.'

A moment later Helen answered: 'Well, the first thing I'd do would be to listen carefully to the parents and find out exactly what they were unhappy about. If they had been misinformed about anything I would clarify what was really happening. I would probably then invite them to spend some time with the class to see for themselves what was happening.'

'Would you not defend your style?'

'If I did *that*, at the beginning, I think it would make them angry. Initially I would want to listen to their point of view. Later I could describe what I did, but not in a defensive way.'

'How would you deal with a really aggressive parent?'

'No differently really; many people are aggressive because they are intimidated by being in a school. By being open and friendly and listening carefully to their problem I would expect to diffuse any anger.'

'You've talked about your strengths, what about your weaknesses?'

'How would you define weaknesses?' Helen asked.

'Things you aren't very good at.'

'I would argue with the word weakness. I consider the things that either I, or the children, don't do well, to be areas of potential to be developed. One area I've been working on recently is my difficulty in refusing requests for help from people. I tend to want to help people and to get involved in a lot of things, and I used to find myself getting overloaded.

However, over the past year I've been learning to say no and to take on only what is sensible. I'm delegating much more now, and learning that I can't always say *yes* and be liked – sometimes I may have to say *no* and be unpopular.'

'Well done,' said Chris, 'you certainly answered those questions well. You dealt very assertively with the difficult questions. I specifically aimed to criticise you, which I did over your teaching style and your lack of management experience in school and in both cases you used negative assertion to agree with what was right then pointed out what I was wrong about.

'I liked the way you handled my question about an aggressive parent. You described how you would take an assertive approach to dealing with it. Are there any particular answers you would like to talk about?'

'Yes, one or two,' replied Helen. 'When you asked me about how I would deal with a complaining parent, I really didn't know what to do because I needed time to think about it.'

'You did just the right thing,' said Chris: 'to say that you wanted time to think is fine.'

'I was also very concerned about how to reply to your question about my weaknesses,' Helen continued. 'This is an attitude of mine that's changed since you began to teach Mark and me about assertiveness and I started avoiding putting myself down. I now encourage the children to think of the things they can't do, as potential for development and so it seemed reasonable to apply this to me too.'

'Quite,' said Chris. 'I don't see anything wrong with challenging a question if it seems appropriate, although how you phrase your answer would need some careful thought. You may have to tone it down for some people.'

'That was really helpful Chris,' said Helen. 'I feel much more confident now. Although I'll still give some thought to other questions they might ask me and how I can answer them.'

'Good luck with the interview,' said Chris warmly. 'If

you think of anything you want to discuss beforehand then just give me a ring.'

*　　*　　*　　*　　*

The following week Helen returned home from the interview quite excited.

'How did it go?' asked Mark.

'Very well,' Helen replied. 'They did ask me some difficult questions but I certainly managed to deal with them assertively. Why don't we go round to the Coach and Horses for supper and we can chat about it?'

Before Mark could reply the phone rang.

'I bet that'll be Chris,' said Helen and went off to answer it.

She returned a moment later. 'Yes it was Chris and I suggested that we all met at the pub for supper.'

'Fine,' said Mark. 'I'll just go and change.'

*　　*　　*　　*　　*

Mark and Helen arrived at the pub and found Chris sitting at a quiet corner table. Chris went to the bar to get drinks while Mark and Helen settled themselves round the table.

'So how did it go?' Chris asked, returning with the drinks.

'Fine,' said Helen, 'although I did have a few difficult moments; luckily though, the practice I had with you had really prepared me for most of the hardest questions.

'You did warn me that they might compliment me as well as criticise, and in fact they complimented me on two occasions. Early on in the interview they said that they had been very impressed by my CV and instead of ignoring it as I would have done a year ago, I was able to say, "Thank you, I put a lot of work into it."

'They asked me about my "weaknesses" and I gave the same answer that I gave you, although, I toned it down

92

a little, and much to my surprise they complimented me on challenging them.

'At one point they threw me a bit by asking me two questions in one. They said "Given the current concern about standards, especially in language and reading, what would be your approach to teaching in this area." I wasn't too sure whether just to wade in with an answer to the first bit about language, but decided to say that I thought they'd asked two very important questions, and which one would they like me to answer first? They seemed quite happy with that.

'The only really difficult time came when they asked me a hypothetical question about whether, if I was restricted in the money I could spend, I would buy a kiln, or a third computer for the school. I decided that a third computer would be more useful than a kiln because we could always use the kiln at the local secondary school.

'One member of the panel then started arguing with me about how a kiln was a much better buy as it could be used by many more children. A year ago I would have probably wavered in my own ideas and agreed with her, but I was able to feel confident in my reply and hold my ground. Afterwards they said that they were interested to see if I could stick to my opinions under pressure and were delighted that I had.'

*   *   *   *   *

The following week Helen came down in the morning to find a letter from the education authority sitting on the mat. She opened it rather nervously and then shouted upstairs to Mark with great excitement.

'Mark, I've got it, I've got the job!'

Mark came rushing downstairs almost falling over in his haste and hugged Helen in delight. 'Well done Helen, I'm so pleased; you deserve it. Let's go out and celebrate tonight.'

93

'That would be nice,' Helen answered. 'You arrange it – I'd like a surprise. I'd better go now or I'll be late for work. I'll be back a little later tonight: I have a meeting straight after school. See you about seven o'clock.'

That evening Helen got home and had just taken her coat off and greeted Mark when the doorbell rang and there stood Chris clutching a bottle of champagne.

'Congratulations Helen, I thought you might like something to celebrate with.'

'Oh, thank you Chris, come in, but how did you know that I'd got the job?'

'Nothing mysterious,' said Chris with a smile. 'Mark phoned me to give me the good news and invited me to join in your celebration.'

'Oh I *am* glad,' Helen replied: 'it wouldn't seem right to celebrate without you. It's mainly due to you and all you've taught me that I got the job.

'Why are we all standing round in the hall?' Mark asked. 'There's a nice fire blazing in the sitting room.'

'Have we time to open the champagne now before we go out?' Helen asked.

'Yes,' Chris replied. 'I'm taking both of you out for dinner tonight to the Pumpkin, the restaurant Mark says you've always wanted to go to. I've booked the table for eight-thirty so we've got time to sit and relax for a while.'

They all made themselves comfortable round the blazing log fire. 'I'd like to propose a toast to you Chris,' said Helen raising her glass. 'With your help I really feel that I'm becoming assertive.'

'I endorse that,' said Mark: 'In many situations I'm now able to behave assertively rather than aggressively, which has made a big difference to my life.'

'To you Chris,' they said, raising their glasses.

'Thank you,' said Chris smiling.

IN WHICH THE TABLES
ARE TURNED

It was just after Christmas and Mark and Helen were driving to visit Mary, an old friend of Helen's.

'I was just thinking then,' said Helen, 'that we visited Mary this time last year, just a short while before Chris started teaching us about assertiveness. Isn't it incredible how our lives have changed? I have a new job, you're getting on with your boss now and you're in line for promotion.'

'I agree,' said Mark. 'If someone had told me what an effect it would have I wouldn't have believed them. I'm particularly amazed at the effect being assertive has had on our relationship. We've even stopped rowing as often as we used to.'

'And,' Helen added, 'the rows we *do* have seem to be so much more constructive. We've got a lot to thank Chris for. It would be nice if one day we got the chance to help someone else by introducing them to assertiveness.'

At that moment they arrived at their destination. Mary welcomed them and they settled down for a pre-lunch drink in Mary's cosy sitting room.

'I got a new toaster for Christmas so I thought I'd try it out and we could have pâté and toast for a starter,' said Mary, and promptly headed off into the kitchen.

Moments later there was a smell of burning toast. 'Having problems?' called Helen.

'The toaster's playing up,' Mary replied. Mark and Helen went into the kitchen to have a look at it.

95

They all looked at the toaster and tried a couple more pieces of bread. 'It does seem to be faulty,' Mary said, sounding gloomy. 'Oh what a nuisance; I hate taking things back to shops: I never know what to say.'

Helen and Mark smiled at each other. 'Funny you should say that,' said Helen, 'I used to have the same problem until I bought a faulty toaster one day, and a friend called Chris taught Mark and I how to be assertive . . . '

HELEN'S SUGGESTED READING LIST

Assert Yourself, Gael Lindenfield, Thorsons.

Assert Yourself, Robert Sharpe, Kogan Page.

Assertiveness at Work, Back K. and K., McGraw Hill.

Assertiveness at Work, David Stubbs, Penguin.

A Woman in Your Own Right, Anne Dixon, Quartet.

Be Assertive, Beverley Hare, Optima.

Don't Say Yes When You Want to Say No, Fensterheim and Baer, Futura.

Getting to Yes, Fisher and Ury, Arrow.

The Aware Manager, Mike Woods, Element.

When I Say No I Feel Guilty, Manuel Smith, Bantam.